The Mystery of Eve and Adam

The Mystery of Eve and Adam
A Prophetic Critique of the Monarchy

Ron Moe-Lobeda

☙PICKWICK *Publications* • Eugene, Oregon

THE MYSTERY OF EVE AND ADAM
A Prophetic Critique of the Monarchy

Copyright © 2012 Ron Moe-Lobeda. All rights reserved. Except for brief quotations in critical publications or reviews, no part of this book may be reproduced in any manner without prior written permission from the publisher. Write: Permissions, Wipf and Stock Publishers, 199 W. 8th Ave., Suite 3, Eugene, OR 97401.

Pickwick Publications
An Imprint of Wipf and Stock Publishers
199 W. 8th Ave., Suite 3
Eugene, OR 97401

www.wipfandstock.com

ISBN 13: 978-1-61097-615-2

Cataloguing-in-Publication data:

Moe-Lobeda, Ron.

    The mystery of Eve and Adam : a prophetic critique of the monarchy / Ron Moe-Lobeda.

    x + 106 p. ; 23 cm. Includes bibliographical references.

    ISBN 13: 978-1-61097-615-2

    1. Bible. O.T. Genesis II–III—Criticism, interpretation, etc. 2. Eve (Biblical figure). 3. Adam (Biblical figure). 4. Kings and ruler—Biblical teaching. I. Title.

BS1237 M64 2012

Manufactured in the U.S.A.

Scripture quotations in this publication are from the New Revised Standard Version of the Bible, copyright © 1989, by the Division of Christian Education of the National Council of the Churches of Christ in the U.S.A.

Cover painting by Xavier Gonzalez d'Egara, *Formazione della conscienza: Adamo/Eva primordiale: Genesis 2:20*, 2011, olio su tavola; 70 x 70 cm. Courtesy of Associazione Culturale Polyhedra—Roma (www.polyhedra.co.cc).

*This book is dedicated to the women of N Street Village,
and all of the women who end up losing their children,
being dominated by men, or being enslaved in a job
as the result of the political, economic, and patriarchal culture
in which they are forced to live.*

Contents

Acknowledgments / ix

Introduction / 1

1. The Lens of Genesis 3:14–19 / 7
2. The Lens of Isaiah 65:17–25 / 19
3. The Lens of Conquest and Deportation / 30
4. The Lens of the Historians / 36
5. The Lens of the Prophets / 42
6. The Lens of Deportation and Return / 49
7. The Lens of Jeremiah / 56
8. The Lens of the Book of Jeremiah / 62
9. The Lenses of History, Politics, and Metaphor / 81

Conclusion / 94

Appendix: The Lens of the Priests / 99

Bibliography / 103

Acknowledgments

This book was the result of three major drafts. The first draft was written during a sabbatical granted by the members of University Lutheran Church in 2004. They granted me another sabbatical in 2011 at which time I completed the third and final draft for this book. I am deeply grateful to the members of this congregation for their generosity, encouragement, and support throughout this entire endeavor. I also thank the readers who gave me valuable feedback and encouragement in this process: Kathleen Kler, Don Mackenzie, Jack Olive, David Swartling, Maynard Atik, Walter Brueggemann, Ched Myers, John Gienapp, Brian Burchfield, Paul Hoffman, Mary Boyd, Erik Wilson Weiberg, and Sinan Demirel.

While on the teaching staff at Holden Village, I had the opportunity for two summers to present this material to enthusiastic audiences who affirmed the importance of publishing this material. I thank my wife, Cynthia, who gave birth to our two dear sons, Leif and Gabe, and supported me throughout this long journey. Finally, I thank my mother who gave birth to me sixty-three years ago and nurtured me along the way and my father who worked by the sweat of his brow at a steel company for thirty-eight years so that I could live comfortably and eat sufficiently every day of my life.

Introduction

THE STORY OF EVE and Adam is one of the most widely interpreted stories in the entire Bible. Everyone has a favorite interpretation of this old familiar tale. Although I have spent the past twenty years searching through the literature related to this story, I have barely scratched the surface of all of the material written about this story of Eve and Adam. Along the way, I have discovered that no one knows for sure who wrote this story, when it was written, and for what purpose it was written.

In his commentary on *Genesis,* Walter Brueggemann has indicated that no text in Genesis (or likely in the entire Bible) has been more used, interpreted, and misunderstood than these two chapters in Genesis.[1] Mary Hayter makes a similar assertion:

> Almost more than any other Old Testament text, these chapters (Genesis 2–3) have undergone a vast range of different interpretations. Scientists and sophists, poets and patristic scholars, rabbis and radical feminists have turned to the text and all too often have made it say only what they want to prove. In fact, the history of interpretation shows how easy it is to press these verses into the service of contemporary philosophical and religious, scientific or romantic thought . . . The fact that interpreters have been too much inclined to read concepts from the anthropological and religious standpoints of their own milieu into the biblical text should prompt modern theologians to seek the meaning of the text in its own context and to ascertain whether there is an abiding theological principle to be deduced from it.[2]

As a result of my research, I have identified many different lenses through which this story has been viewed and interpreted throughout the ages. Some of the more familiar lenses are: allegorical, anthropological, archaeological, archetypal, cosmological, developmental, doctrinal, eco-

---

1. Brueggemann, *Genesis,* 41.
2. Hayter, *The New Eve,* 95–96.

logical, environmental, epistemological, eschatological, ethical, etiological, evangelical, exegetical, geological, historical, ideological, linguistical, literal, metaphorical, moral, mythological, natural, personal, phenomenological, philological, philosophical, political, psychoanalytical, psychological, psycho-spiritual, relational, rhetorical, sexual, socio-historical, sociological, spiritual, and theological.

As Hayter points out, many of these lenses have been used by people to make this story of Eve and Adam say what they want for whatever reason they want. Consequently, this story has been used to explain the origin of human life on this earth, to describe how man and woman came into being, to articulate the relationships between men and women, to portray the origin of sin in this world, to describe how God responded to the first humans' disobedience, to present the consequences of a fallen humanity, and to explain the reason for death in this life. At the heart of most of these interpretations is the assumption that this story of Eve and Adam is a creation story—a story in which the primary purpose for humanity of tilling the land is explained, the need for human companionship is determined, the institution of marriage is established, and the reasons for serpents crawling on their bellies, women experiencing pain in childbirth, and men being obligated to work every day of their lives are all explained.

The interpretation of this story that I offer in this book assumes none of the above. Instead, after many years of asking provocative questions, being open to new insights, listening to vital clues, and following sensible leads, I have ended up seeing and hearing this story through the lenses of history, politics, and metaphor. I am not the first person to use these lenses for the interpretation of this story. According to Terje Stordalen, the story of Eve and Adam has a definite historical context. He offers several possibilities for the inclusion of this story in the Hebrew Bible. Along with expressing an early worldview for the children of Israel, this story could be a commentary on portions of the Deuteronomistic History, a comparison between Eden and Zion, an archetype for the Jerusalem temple, a religio-political cosmogony to establish Israel's right to the land, a judgment against foreign religions, a judgment against the Yahwistic cult, an ideological legitimacy for Davidic rule, a warning against ambitious politics, a reflection of the common royal politic, or a critique of contemporary politics.[3]

3. Stordalen, *Echoes of Eden*, 306–17.

As if these possibilities were not enough, authors such as Elaine Pagels,[4] Alice Bellis,[5] John Phillips,[6] Jean Delumeau,[7] Gerard Luttikhuizen,[8] and Kristen Kvam, Linda Schearing, and Valerie Zieglar[9] have reviewed how this story or certain characters in this story have been interpreted throughout the ages, including interpretations by the rabbis prior to the first century of the Common Era, by Jesus of Nazareth, and by early Christian writers. I have no illusion to think that I could adequately review the vast array of interpretations of Gen 2:4b—3:24 that have been proposed since this story was authored. The above-mentioned authors, as well as others, have accomplished this task quite well. However, even after reading through all of these summations of interpretations, I am convinced that this story of Eve and Adam still offers another perspective that can be ascertained through the lenses of history, politics, and metaphor.

Given all of the different interpretations of this story, I have drawn upon one of the very first principles of interpretation that I was taught in order to see and hear this story in a new light. The principle is known as *scripture interpreting scripture*. According to this principle, when one passage or story in the Bible has so many different interpretations, a person can examine other portions of scripture in order to gain some clarity about the passage or story in question. Utilizing this principle with the story of Eve and Adam, I have come to understand this story through the composite history of Israel and Judah as well as through the imagination of the prophets, particularly as recorded in the book of Third Isaiah (Isaiah 56–66) and the book of Jeremiah.

Joel Rosenberg offers a keen insight into this particular approach to this story of Eve and Adam. He states:

> The makers of biblical literature were not solely concerned with advancing a particular view of God, or religious ritual, or moral law; on another plane, they were not solely concerned with telling a good story. Rather they were deeply pre-occupied with the nature of Israel's political community and were interested in the

4. Pagels, *Adam, Eve and the Serpent*.
5. Bellis, *Helpmates, Harlots and Heroes*.
6. Phillips, *Eve: The History of an Idea*.
7. Delumeau, *History of Paradise*.
8. Luttikhuizen, *The Creation of Man and Woman*.
9. Kvam, et al., *Eve and Adam*.

> premises of political existence, addressing themselves to readers who thought about such things as leadership, authority, social cohesiveness, political order, rebellion, crime, justice, institutional evolution, and the relation of rich and poor . . . Biblical thought is rooted in its time and place, and, as such, is addressed to a particular kind of reader, one willing to undertake the deeply philosophical task of knowing "Israel" in all her dimensions. As such, this reader must be willing to ask what forces lead or divide the members of a political community—from the smallest scope of household and family, to the wider scope of village, tribe, and tribal confederation, to the widest scope of nation-state and kingdom.[10]

Consistent with Rosenberg's viewpoint, I offer an interpretation of this story that takes into account both the historical context and the political message that too often have been overlooked by most of the interpretations projected onto this story. Many of these interpretations attempt to extract a meaning out of every detail of this story, often forcing the story to say more than what the authors intended to convey. Drawing upon Rosenberg's assertion that there are stories in which every element has a meaning, and there are stories in which only some of the elements are meaningful,[11] I have taken the latter approach to this story of Eve and Adam.

While the primary interpretations of this story historically have offered reasonable explanations about the author, the date, and the intention of this story, each interpretation has left me with some major questions unanswered in this regard. This book presents to the reader the inquisitive process by which I have come to this particular interpretation of the story of Eve and Adam and invites the reader on a journey that will offer another possibility regarding the authorship, date, and purpose of this story. This journey did not begin with a hypothesis that I had to prove or disprove, but rather began with a simple question that culminated in an interpretation of this story of Eve and Adam that makes the most sense to me.

The primary question that initiated this process for me was related to the phrase in Gen 3:16 in which God tells the woman that she will experience pain in bringing forth children. Having been skeptical most

---

10. Rosenberg, *King and Kin*, x.
11. Ibid., 44.

of my life about the usual explanation that the pain in this verse refers to the physical pain that a woman must experience in giving birth to a child, I always wondered, "Could the pain mentioned in this verse refer to something other than the physical pain of giving birth?" This question laid the foundation for many more questions about the meaning of Gen 3:14–19 until I finally realized that I had to deal with the entire story of Eve and Adam.

Expanding my inquiry beyond these illustrious six verses, I soon discovered that this story presented a synopsis of the historical narrative regarding Israel and Judah. The story ends with the deportation of the people of Judah to Babylon. In light of this discovery, I realized that the story of Eve and Adam was a description of the monarchies of Israel and Judah, and explained the reason for the pain that the woman felt in giving birth within this political environment. The same explanation would hold true for the man who had to labor in order to put food on his table.

Consequently, I finally concluded that this story probably was written after the people of Judah were deported to Babylon in order to dissuade the people from reinstating any form of a monarchy that resembled the kings who had ruled over Israel and Judah prior to the conquest by the Babylonians. As far as the authors of this story were concerned, the reinstatement of the monarchy would result in the renewal of an increase in the infant mortality rate, greater subjugation of women throughout the land, and the enslavement of the people of the land for the benefit of the king and all of the landowners who would be loyal to the king. Under the previous monarchies in both Israel and Judah, all three of these benchmarks were evident in the downfall of these two nations. The authors of this story of Eve and Adam wanted to make sure that such a government was not reinstated so that the people would not have to suffer through these consequences ever again. Who these authors are also became apparent as I continued on this journey of inquiry and discovery.

In order to guide the readers of this book through this journey, chapter 1 reviews some of the primary interpretations of Gen 3:14–19. Chapter 2 examines these verses through the lens of Isa 65:17–25. Chapter 3 suggests that the date for the story of Eve and Adam can be determined through the lens of the conquest and deportation of the people of Judah. Chapter 4 uses the lens of the historical account of Israel and Judah in order to view the entire story of Eve and Adam. Chapter 5 examines what happened during the monarchy through the lens of the prophets. Chapter

6 returns to the period when the people return from Babylon and determine how they will live into the future. Chapter 7 draws upon the experience of Jeremiah and his followers as a lens for understanding the reason this story was told. Chapter 8 compares the content of the story of Eve and Adam with the content of the book of Jeremiah in order to demonstrate that the followers of Jeremiah could have been the authors of this story. Chapter 9 utilizes all of these connections to offer a new interpretation of this story of Eve and Adam as seen through the primary lenses of history, politics, and metaphor—the ultimate metaphor being that Eve and Adam actually represent Israel and Judah in this story.

1

The Lens of Genesis 3:14–19

The LORD God said to the serpent, "Because you have done this, cursed are you among all animals and among all wild creatures; upon your belly you shall go, and dust you shall eat all the days of your life. I will put enmity between you and the woman, and between your offspring and hers; he will strike your head, and you will strike his heel." To the woman the Lord God said, "I will greatly increase your pangs in childbearing; in pain you shall bring forth children, yet your desire shall be for your husband, and he shall rule over you." And to the man the LORD God said, "Because you have listened to the voice of your wife, and have eaten of the tree about which I commanded you, 'You shall not eat of it,' cursed is the ground because of you; in toil you shall eat of it all the days of your life; thorns and thistles it shall bring forth for you; and you shall eat the plants of the field. By the sweat of your face you shall eat bread until you return to the ground, for out of it you were taken; you are dust, and to dust you shall return."

As a young boy, I was taught that the physical pain that my mother experienced when she gave birth to me was the result of Eve's disobedience and was evidence of the sinfulness of humankind. Similarly, I learned that the reason that my father had to work so hard in order to put food on our table was based upon the fact that Adam disobeyed God and ate the fruit from the forbidden tree in the Garden of Eden. For most of my life, I felt uneasy about this explanation for the physical pain that women experience in childbirth and the labor that men have to endure in order to make a living. Consequently, twenty years ago, I began to search through the literature pertaining to these statements in Genesis 3, only to discover that for almost 2,200 years, no matter how differently scholars have interpreted this story, most scholars have deviated very little from this explanation about the cause of this pain and labor in the story of Eve and Adam.

One of the most important distinctions among all of these different explanations is whether or not these experiences of the woman and the man in Genesis 3 are prescriptive or descriptive. If they are prescriptive, then the pain for women in giving birth and the labor for men in earning a living have been determined by God as a result of human disobedience. A prescriptive interpretation of these experiences often assumes that prior to human disobedience, this pain and labor were non-existent in God's creation. If these verses about the pain of women and the labor of men are descriptive, then they reflect the real conditions that exist in this world without attributing them to any specific cause. From this perspective, God is portrayed as describing how things are in this world as opposed to stating how things have to be. Not every interpretation of these six verses in Genesis 3 fits neatly into these two categories. However, most scholars tend to interpret the pain for women in giving birth and the labor for men in earning a living either prescriptively or descriptively.

PRESCRIPTIVE INTERPRETATIONS

Augustine is one of the best examples in setting the tone for a prescriptive interpretation of these experiences described in Genesis 3. He insisted that through an act of will, Eve and Adam did change the structure of the universe. By their single, willful act, human nature, as well as nature in general, was corrupted permanently. He believed that once-upon-a-time women could experience painless childbearing, but as punishment for Eve's willful disobedience, all women suffer nausea, illness, and pains of pregnancy as well as the painful contractions of parturition that accompany normal labor. According to Augustine, as a result of Eve's disobedience, not only do many women experience the greater agonies of miscarriage, tortures inflicted by doctors, or the shock and loss of giving birth to an infant stillborn or moribund, many women also give birth to a child that is blind, deaf, deformed, without the use of limbs, insane, or afflicted with a chronic or fatal disease. Similarly, when Adam sinned, all nature was changed for the worse. God originally placed the man in Eden in order to till the soil and cultivate it without any labor, but as a result of Adam's disobedience, every man has to experience pain, frustration, and hardship in his labor.[1] John Chrysostrom reinforced this perspective by stating that every time that a woman gives birth to a child, the pain is the personal reminder of the magnitude of Eve's sin of disobedience, never to be forgotten. The only thing that will balance this pain is the satisfaction of bearing a child.[2]

Martin Luther tried to look on the bright side of this punishment by insisting that in spite of Eve's disobedience, women get to keep the blessing of a sexual relationship, procreation, and motherhood. However, as far as the entire process of conception and birth is concerned, the joy of procreation is threatened by headaches, dizziness, nausea, loathing of food and drink, vomiting, stomach disorder, and cravings. In addition to the physical pain of giving birth, the distress that women felt about whether or not they would survive the process of childbirth also was a woman's punishment for Eve's disobedience. Similarly, Luther acknowledged that before Adam sinned, no part of the earth was barren or inferior. However, as a result of sin, the earth became barren, was defaced with weeds, thorns, and thistles, and made life hard for the farmer. In fact, with the increase of sin, God's punishment included diseases, frost, lightning, storms, floods, hail, and even earthquakes.[3]

This prescriptive interpretation of these experiences of the woman and the man in Genesis 3 is not limited to theologians from centuries ago. Modern scholars also reflect this theology no matter whether they believe that Eve and Adam are real historical figures or believe that they represent all women and men throughout human history. A few examples of this modern-day interpretation of the pain of women and the labor of men as described in Genesis 3 will suffice in demonstrating that this understanding about the consequences of human sin is still alive in our modern society.

According to Charles Aalder, the physical pain for women in giving birth is the punishment for Eve's disobedience.[4] David Cline states that God severely punished Eve by promising to make the one thing that she had been created to do difficult for her. As a childbearing creature, Eve would have to suffer pain in childbirth as often as she conceives and

---

1. Augustine, *Opus Imperfectum*, 133–34.
2. Chrysostrom, *Homilies in Genesis*, 146.
3. Luther, *Lectures on Genesis*, 199–201, 205–6.
4. Aalders, *Genesis*, 108.

carries the baby to full term.[5] Susan Foh claims that experiencing pain in giving birth describes the result of the fall and the consequences of sin that have subverted the created order forever.[6] According to Mary Hayter, childbearing itself is not a punishment for sin, but the consequence of this transgression is the increase of pain in bringing forth the fruits of the body.[7] William Phipps concludes that the consequence of Eve's misuse of moral freedom is the pain that she must endure in childbirth.[8] Adrien Bledstein points out that to an ancient audience, increased pain in her capacity to procreate might seem an appropriate punishment for this woman who aspired to be a goddess.[9]

Many scholars accept that pain is the consequence of Eve's disobedience, but offer a broader understanding regarding the realm of this pain. Harold Stigers expands upon the physical pain of childbearing to include other trials and even death itself as the result of Eve's sin.[10] Allen Ross indicates that the word for pain may not be limited to the physical suffering in the process of childbirth, but also may include emotional pain as well.[11] Margaret Hammar goes one step further and states that the downside of childbearing is the taxing labor, as well as the physical, emotional, and spiritual distress.[12] James Boice carries the pain of childbirth into the role of being a parent by suggesting that Eve's punishment also includes the pain of having a child who is disobedient and makes the parent's life a living hell.[13] Even with these broader interpretations of a woman's pain, the physical pain of giving birth still is assumed to be the consequence of Eve's disobedience.

According to this prescriptive perspective, the other consequence of Eve's disobedience is the subjugation that women have to endure in relation to their husbands even though they still have a desire to be with their husbands. Chrysostrom indicates that Eve was created equal with man, but she abused her status and demonstrated that she did not know how

5. Clines, *What Does Eve Do?* 35.
6. Foh, "Woman's Desire," 382–83.
7. Hayter, *The New Eve*, 107.
8. Phipps, *Genesis and Gender*, 51.
9. Bledstein, "Are Women Cursed?" 142–43.
10. Stigers, *Commentary on Genesis*, 80.
11. Ross, *Creation and Blessing*, 146.
12. Hammar, *Giving Birth*, 30.
13. Boice, *Genesis*, 178.

to rule. Therefore, she would have to be subject to her husband and learn how to be ruled by her master for her own protection.[14] Luther attributes this relationship of domination and subjugation to Eve's unfaithfulness. "Eve is placed under the power of her husband. Previously she had been free and the recipient of all of the gifts of God and in no way inferior to her husband. The rule remains with the husband and the wife is compelled to obey him by God's command . . . If Eve had remained faithful, she would have been a partner in the rule of her husband which is now entirely the concern of males."[15]

This perspective has been supported by modern scholars who tend to justify male domination over their wives. Isaac Asimov states this position as bluntly as anyone. "Male domination is justified here as a punishment for the woman because she yielded first to the temptation."[16] H. C. Leupold states that when Eve tried to act independently of Adam and sought to take control of the situation and sinned, God took that control away from her so that her husband could exercise control over her.[17] While Aalders claims that Eve was the one responsible for disturbing the harmonious relationship between the man and the woman,[18] Hayter makes a direct correlation between Eve's disobedience and the subservience of the woman to her husband.[19] Boice indicates that Eve and all women after her may not be willing to accept this subservient role. As a result of sin, the woman will resist God's judgment and will desire to control her husband so that the husband will be forced to fight for his headship as ordained by God.[20] Danna Fewell and David Gunn conclude that the woman's desire for her husband is the punishment that will subordinate her to the man and set the stage for the hierarchical priority of the man in this world.[21]

The same rationale for the consequences of Adam's disobedience is explained by many scholars today. According to Ross, men have to experience painful toil in order to eat because Adam ate the fruit from the for-

---

14. Chrysostom, *Homilies on Genesis*, 146.
15. Luther, *Lectures on Genesis*, 202–3.
16 Asimov, *In the Beginning*, 114.
17. Leupold, *Exposition of Genesis*, 172.
18. Aalders, *Genesis*, 108–9.
19. Hayter, *The New Eve*, 107.
20. Boice, *Genesis*, 178–79.
21. Fewell and Gunn, *Gender*, 36–37.

bidden tree. God cursed the ground as a physical reminder of man's sin.[22] Phipps states that man's disobedience of God's command alienated man from God and caused this disharmony in earthly associations that would result in work being a given struggle with nature.[23] Leupold indicates that as a result of man's submission to Eve's offering, man will experience subordination to the soil over which he once had complete control.[24] Nahum Sarna concludes that as a result of man's transgression, the very matter from which man originated has turned against him so that all humans now are condemned to a ceaseless and brutal struggle for subsistence.[25] John Davies states that Adam's disobedience has spoiled the once friendly relationship between man and the ground and will mean that the soil will yield so little reward that men will always feel discouraged because their efforts to provide nourishment for themselves and their families will never be sufficient or worthwhile.[26] Donald Gowan recalls that work originally was a blessing of God in creation, but as a result of God's curse, the ground produces adequate food for people only through the most strenuous and unending exertion that is fraught with futility, uncertainty of results, and a drudgery that often brings forth little of value.[27]

Of course, the serpent does not escape punishment in this prescriptive interpretation. As a result of tempting Eve to eat from the tree of life, the serpent will have to crawl on its belly, eat dust, and suffer the consequences of humiliation,[28] abomination,[29] and frustration,[30] for the rest of its days. Leupold argues that the more serious aspect of the serpent's punishment is the enmity that is created between the serpent and the woman, which represents an enmity between two morally responsible agents.[31] Other scholars pick up on this understanding and interpret this enmity as the perpetual conflict between good and evil until the seed of

---

22. Ross, *Creation and Blessing*, 147.
23. Phipps, *Genesis and Gender*, 51–52.
24. Leupold, *Exposition of Genesis*, 174.
25. Sarna, *Genesis*, 28.
26. Davies, *Beginning Now*, 232–33.
27. Gowan, *From Eden to Babel*, 59–60.
28. Sarna, *Genesis*, 27.
29. Cassuto, *Book of Genesis*, 159.
30. Boice, *Genesis*, 159.
31. Leupold, *Exposition of Genesis*, 164.

the woman triumphs,[32] and man no longer is lured away from God by the temptations of this force of evil, otherwise known as Satan or the devil.[33]

Once the serpent is described as being Satan, the punishment of the serpent in Gen 3:15 takes on a whole new meaning in the history of the church. Stigers claims that this verse has become the most important verse in the entire Bible, because it is the foundation of all faith and the enunciator of the incarnation and resurrection of Jesus Christ, who will trample Satan just as the serpent has trampled on Eve and Adam.[34] This interpretation of Gen 3:15 has been given the name of *protevangelium*, because, as Davies claims, this verse is the first intimation of the Gospel when Christ will come to claim victory over Satan.[35] The victory in this conflict is not won by the collective seed of the woman, but rather by the one unique seed of the woman that is our Lord Jesus Christ and by him alone.[36] As the first messianic prophecy, this prophecy is fulfilled when Satan bruises Jesus' heel on the cross, but then is bruised by Jesus when Jesus is raised by God from the dead. When this happened, Satan would realize that this curse by a punitive God would be fulfilled as the all-wise God had predicted this victory already at the beginning of time.[37]

This summary of the prescriptive interpretations of Gen 3:14–19 indicates how many scholars have matter-of-factly assumed the direct correlation between Eve and Adam's disobedience and the reality of physical pain in giving birth, of domination in human relationships, and of the constant struggle in earning a living. From this perspective, the serpent also does not escape punishment, no matter whether the serpent is perceived to be part of the natural world or is identified as the personification of evil in the spiritual realm. This reality of sin and evil creates the need for both a savior and another world where there will be no more pain and suffering. As long as there is another world to anticipate, the cause of this pain in giving birth, this labor of putting food on the table, and this strain in our human relationships as well as in our relationship with the animal kingdom does not have to be called into question. Although God's judg-

32. Ross, *Creation and Blessing*, 142.
33. Fretheim, *Creation*, 88.
34. Stigers, *Commentary on Genesis*, 79.
35. Davies, *Beginning Now*, 227.
36. Aalders, *Genesis*, 106.
37. Boice, *Genesis*, 164–65.

ment may seem rather harsh in this story, God's grace is made manifest in the promise that the woman's seed will produce a savior who eventually will defeat the serpent and restore all of God's disrupted creative order back to its original harmonious existence where there will be no more pain in childbirth, no more domination by men over women, no more undue labor in growing crops, and no more death. However, until this time comes, human beings are further punished and consigned to endure the consequences of their sin by being expelled from the garden.

After reviewing all of these prescriptive interpretations of these six verses, and many more like them, I was left with some nagging questions. Why would anyone suggest that these verses were a prescription for the way things have to be for all time as if a woman's physical pain in giving birth, a woman's subjugation to her husband, or a man's physical labor in putting food on the table was ordained and instituted by God? How could anyone think that these conditions of our human life actually are God's punishment for the sins that our ancestors committed, and for the sins that we continue to commit to this very day? Does this prescriptive interpretation presume that we could return to the way that God originally created the world if we could be completely obedient to God's will? Besides, is this the image of God that I want to convey to my children and my children's children—a God who punishes all of humankind for the sins of a couple of characters who lived a long, long time ago? One response to all of these questions is to view these verses descriptively.

DESCRIPTIVE INTERPRETATIONS

Theologians who prefer to view these verses descriptively argue that the author is attempting to describe the conditions of the time when this story was being told and perhaps written down. Consequently, this description reflects the physical pain that women actually experience when giving birth to a baby, and the desire that women have for their husbands in spite of being dominated by their husbands. This description also reflects the challenge that men have to face in growing food for themselves and their families until the day that they die. Even God's curse on the serpent in Gen 3:14 falls into this descriptive category as the author of this story explains how and why the serpent crawls on its belly and eats the dust of the ground all the days of its life. A sampling of scholars will demonstrate the popularity of this descriptive interpretation of Gen 3:14–19.

Carol Meyers argues that these verses have nothing to do with sin, but rather serve as a divine sanction for conditions as they are and reflect the harsh agrarian life during the early years of Israel's settlement in the promised land. Reflecting upon the demanding role that women had to play in this agrarian society, Meyers suggests that God's curse on the woman be translated to read: "I will greatly increase your toil and your pregnancies and with travail you shall beget children." With this translation, Meyers emphasizes the increase in physical labor for women, not their pain, as well as the process of raising children, not giving them birth. Meyers also argues that God's statement to the man in Genesis 3 is an accurate description about the experience of the farmer during this period of Israel's history in terms of the labor that was necessary to produce food for the household as well as in terms of the inevitability of death itself.[38]

According to Thomas Thompson, this fictional story is not an explanation about original sin, good and evil, or a rivalry between God and Satan, but rather is a description about the present reality of life when this story was written and explains a truth about being human at any time in human history.[39] Helen Schungel-Strauman agrees that this story is not an explanation about the origin of sin, but rather portrays the reality of life and explains the reason for the pain of childbirth, the disharmony of the relationship between the sexes, and the hard work in the field.[40] John Scullion contends that there never was a time in human history when the serpent did not move on its belly, when childbirth was painless, when domestic subjection was non-existent, and when the ground did not produce weeds in order to make the farmer sweat at his work.[41]

Claus Westermann states that this description explains the natural hostility between snakes and human beings, the destiny of women who are assigned pain in giving birth to children, and the reality of men who have to eke out a living from their labor on the land—labor from which there was no escape.[42] Bruce Vawter adds to this list by stating that the hostility between the snake and the human as well as the hostility in the marital relationship are reflective of the state of affairs when this story

38. Meyers, *Discovering Eve*, 84, 90.
39. Thompson, *The Mythic Past*, 83–88.
40. Schungel-Strauman, "Man and Woman," 66–70.
41. Scullion, *Genesis*, 40–42.
42. Westermann, *Genesis 1–11*, 256–67.

originated.⁴³ Affirming the descriptive nature of this story, Leon Kass states that this story illuminates the fundamental and universal features of human sexuality, the nature of man and woman, and the natural basis of their complicated relationship.⁴⁴ Dorothee Soelle lends a hopeful note to this perspective by stating that this description presents the inevitable reality of life for the woman and the man, but is not prescriptive for the way things have to be forever.⁴⁵ Likewise, Phyllis Trible views these verses as God's protest against what is wrong in the universe in the hope that the erotic relationships and activity of creation might be restored.⁴⁶

The perspective that these verses are descriptive of the reality of the society at the time when this story was told or written actually makes much more sense to me. However, when someone suggests that the physical pain of giving birth and the physical labor of earning a living are descriptive of the way things are in the world, is that person implying that there may come a day when women will be able to give birth without any physical pain or when men will be able to put food on the table without having to work as hard as they do? Even if these verses are descriptive of our reality, I still was left wondering, "Have these experiences always been the reality of humankind? If not, then how did we come to know such pain and labor in our lives? Besides, why should such natural dimensions of our human life be portrayed in such a negative way in the first place? If these descriptions of childbirth and daily work are considered God's curse upon humanity, then where is the joy in giving birth and in working to put food on the table?"

ALTERNATIVE INTERPRETATIONS

Not feeling completely satisfied with either of these two major interpretations of Gen 3:14–19, I was drawn to those scholars who attributed this story of Eve and Adam to what may have been happening under the monarchy that was established when David was appointed by God to rule over Israel and Judah. Whereas James Kennedy explains that this story legitimates the power and domination of the monarchy in order to maintain control over a peasantry that is dissatisfied and threatens the

---

43. Vawter, *On Genesis*, 82–85.
44. Kass, *The Beginning of Wisdom*, 99.
45. Soelle, *The Strength of the Weak*, 128.
46. Trible, *Rhetoric of Sexuality*, 125.

state's status quo,⁴⁷ Harold Bloom and David Rosenberg explain that this story is a description not about the fall of man and woman that results in a sentence of death, but rather about the decline of the Davidic kingdom during which time women experienced physical pain while giving birth and men had to endure the drudgery of hard labor in order to put food on the table.⁴⁸

Robert Coote and David Ord offer an historical perspective of these verses that recalls the time when the children of Israel enjoyed the harmony, peace, and prosperity of David's reign. However, as the powerful elite seized more and more control of the land, forced people to form collectives in order to farm the land, and taxed the people on a collective basis for using the land, everything that was intended to be good about David's kingdom deteriorated into nothing but a toilsome and painful endeavor just to put food on the table. Only when the powerful elite died would the peasants be free to return to this vision of the peaceable kingdom.⁴⁹

Edward Conklin takes a much more global perspective of the presence of the serpent in this story and states that the imagery of the serpent hearkens back to the ancient Sumerian tale of a garden paradise in which the primal deity worshiped by the people was the serpent Ea. Since the serpent Ea was so well-known throughout the Mediterranean world, the image may well have inspired the appearance of the serpent in this story of Eve and Adam. Conklin further explains that as males began to understand their role in sexual reproduction, they saw themselves as the dominant sex and incorporated this view into this story as a way to substantiate the move from a matriarchy in early Hebrew life to a patriarchy.⁵⁰

In addition to her descriptive perspective, Meyers also contends that this creation story reflects the gender balance of responsibility in early Israel and portrays an ideology of humanitarian and egalitarian principles unique to Israel as it broke away from the socio-political systems of the Canaanites and Egyptians who dominated that part of the world.⁵¹ Lyn Bechtel emphasizes that during this period of human history, the woman had to increase giving birth in order to produce enough children to work

---

47. Kennedy, "Peasants in Revolt," 3–10.
48. Bloom and Rosenberg, *The Book of J*, 184–87.
49. Coote and Ord, *Bible's First History*, 63.
50. Conklin, *Back into the Garden*, 44–47, 104.
51. Meyers, *Discovering Eve*, 9.

on the farm, although she always ran the risk of dying in the process. Therefore, the risk for women in giving birth, the relationship of husband and wife, and the role of men in growing food were all necessary for the survival of the clan.[52]

Many scholars conclude from God's curse on the serpent in this story that the story of Eve and Adam is a condemnation of the Canaanite religions that subverted the monotheism of Israel. Terence Fretheim explains that as the Israelites established themselves in the land of Canaan, they often were tempted by the religious practices of the Canaanites who worshiped serpents as symbols of the deity.[53] Norman Habel corroborates this perspective by stating that the presentation of the snake in this story is a polemic against the indigenous Canaanite religions of the region.[54] Peter Ellis states that the serpent almost certainly symbolizes the Canaanite fertility religions because the seduction of Israel by these fertility cults is the fundamental sin of Israel.[55]

Given all of these various interpretations of Gen 3:14–19, I still was left wondering, "No matter whether an author views these verses as prescriptive or descriptive, or offers some alternative explanation for these curses, almost everyone consistently assumes that the pain of childbirth in Gen 3:16 refers to the physical pain of giving birth to a baby. Similarly, the labor of tilling the ground in Gen 3:17–18 refers to the daily struggle of growing food to feed a family. Is there some other explanation for these curses that everyone is missing? After all of this review, how do I deal with my uneasiness that still persists about this traditional explanation for the pain in childbirth and the labor in the production of food?" There had to be some other explanation for the pain that a woman experiences in giving birth other than being the physical pain that women generally experience at this time in their lives.

---

52. Bechtel, "Rethinking the Interpretation," 104–5.
53. Fretheim, *Creation*, 80–85.
54. Habel, *The Fall Narrative*, 14.
55. Ellis, *The Yahwist*, 62–64.

2

The Lens of Isaiah 65:17–25

MUCH OF MY MUSING about these six verses in Genesis 3 occurred while I was serving as a pastor at Luther Place Memorial Church in Washington, DC—a congregation that decided in the late 1970s to open the doors of the church to homeless women and become a place of refuge and hospitality for them. This ministry with homeless women became known as N Street Village, and offered a full continuum of care for any woman who knocked at the door. During my ten years at Luther Place, I was asked by the staff of N Street Village to facilitate a spirituality group for women in recovery from alcohol and drug abuse, and offer the women an opportunity to talk about their journeys in the context of their faith and life in the Spirit. After two months of becoming acquainted with the women and reassuring them that I was not there to convert them to Lutheranism, I settled into a weekly routine of reading a story of Jesus' encounter with women in the Bible and using these stories as a catalyst for the women to share their own stories.

As I listened to their stories, I was amazed at how any of these women could have survived the traumatic and painful ordeals of their lives, especially as they suffered at the hands of other people or powers in their lives. I heard about their pain of being raped by a father, an uncle, or a mother's boyfriend. I heard about their pain of being dominated and physically abused by a boyfriend or a husband. Occasionally, some of the women would talk about how they were forced by their pastor to stand up in front of a congregation and confess their sins of sexual promiscuity for which they had been accused.

Many of these women turned to drugs during their adolescence in order to escape the horrendous reality of their lives. Once addicted, they often had two choices in order to support their habit—become a prostitute or become a thief, or both. The first choice often resulted in the harsh life of working for a domineering pimp and sacrificing one's body to serve a predominantly male clientele. The second choice generally led to an arrest, a conviction, and a jail sentence that only hardened the women in becoming more proficient and effective as they returned to their former habits. I listened as these women talked about the pain of all of their experiences that often culminated in becoming homeless and having to learn how to survive on the streets of the city.

However, no matter how painful any of these experiences may have been, the worst pain for most of these women was the pain of knowing that their decisions and actions had separated them from their children to whom they had given birth. Often as a result of being a drug addict, turning tricks as a prostitute, serving time in prison, or living on the streets as a homeless person, a woman who had given birth to any child was forced to put her child into the foster care system or relinquish the responsibility of raising her child to another relative. If a woman became pregnant during this period of her life, she often was faced with the painful decision of putting her baby up for adoption or of aborting the fetus because she knew that she was unable to raise a child in her condition.

Although the women who were sharing these stories took full responsibility for their decisions and actions, I often wondered what role our government and our entire country had played in perpetuating the conditions of poverty that often held these women captive as well as enslaved them to the men in their lives. I also wondered how the lives of the children of these women might have been different had their mothers had the proper resources to raise their children. Although I heard very few stories from these women about any of their children dying prematurely as a result of the circumstances of their lives, many of them talked about their pain of not having adequate resources to feed their children or of not being able to afford proper healthcare for themselves and their children.

In the course of these conversations, I had the opportunity to prepare a study on the book of Isaiah for the members of Luther Place, and was drawn to the description in Isa 65:17–25 about the new heavens and a new earth that would be created by God. In this new creation, the sound of weeping or the cry of distress would be heard no more. No infant would die prematurely or unnecessarily due to the neglect or abuse of another person. Under normal circumstances, everyone would be able to live out a lifetime. In this new creation, no one would have to build a house for another person to inhabit or plant a vineyard that someone else owned. Instead, all people would be able to build and inhabit their own houses and eat the fruit from their own vineyards. Most significantly, in this new creation, no one would labor in vain or bear children for calamity. At the conclusion of this text, the peace of this new creation is described by the wolf and the lamb feeding together and by the lion eating straw like an ox. However, the author also points out that the food of the serpent would be dust.

As I read this passage again, I had an "ah-ha" moment and realized that this comment about the serpent eating dust in Isaiah 65 was very similar to the curse that God placed on the serpent in Gen 3:14. Once I took note of this connection between Isaiah 65 and Genesis 3, I began to wonder if the interpretation of Isaiah 65 might offer any new insight into my questions about the meaning of the curses by God in Gen 3:14–19 that are addressed to the serpent, the woman, and the man. In particular, could the sound of weeping and cry of distress in Isaiah 65 offer a new explanation for the pain that the woman was supposed to experience in bringing forth children as described in Gen 3:16? If the pain of bearing children in Isaiah 65 was the pain of knowing that a newborn child would face certain calamity and even death due to the political and economic conditions of the day, then perhaps this same circumstance was the primary cause of pain for the woman in Gen 3:16.

This connection between the cry of distress in Isaiah 65 and the pain mentioned in Gen 3:16 led me to wonder if the same connection could be made between Isaiah 65 and Gen 3:17–19 in which the man is told by God that he would have to work by the sweat of his brow for the rest of his days. What if this description in Isaiah 65 about one person building a house for another person to inhabit or planting a vineyard for the benefit of another person was the same situation being described in Genesis 3, except with different words? At the time, the description in Isaiah 65 sounded to me like some form of forced labor or slavery. If so, then could God's statement to the man in Gen 3:17–19 actually be a description of the oppression and slavery that some men experience and often would result in certain death? If so, then is this description in Genesis 3 referring to some universal condition of humankind or to some particular period of history in which slavery was experienced or remembered by the authors of both of these passages?

With all of these questions racing through my mind, I began to wonder if both of these passages were reflecting the same experience of the monarchies of Israel and Judah—the six verses in Genesis 3 describing the conditions that existed under these monarchies and the passage in Isaiah 65 anticipating a new way of life that would be different from what people had experienced under the previous monarchies. Once I opened the door to this possibility that the description in Gen 3:14–19 was about conditions under the monarchies, I asked myself, "Could the entire story of Eve and Adam be a commentary on these monarchies?"

Once I posed this question, the history of Israel and Judah, with which I was so familiar, unfolded before my very eyes as I considered the entire story of Eve and Adam—how Israel and Judah were situated in the promised land, how the elders decided to have a king like other nations in lieu of God being the king of the people, how the oppression, enslavement, and death of the people increased under the monarchy, and how the people of Israel and Judah were deported from their land just as Eve and Adam were expelled from the Garden of Eden. Could it be that this story of Eve and Adam wasn't meant to be an explanation about the origin of life, but rather was descriptive about what the people had experienced under the monarchy—an experience that they would rather not repeat? If so, then perhaps this story of Eve and Adam originated sometime after the people of Judah had experienced the conquest by the Babylonians and the subsequent deportation that forced so many of their people to live in a foreign land.

Before I proceeded to pursue this possible interpretation of the story of Eve and Adam, I knew that I had to get a better understanding of the context for Isa 65:17–25. One thing I knew for sure! When these two passages from Isaiah 65 and Genesis 3 were put side-by-side, the similarity of imagery was phenomenal, culminating in the similar statement that the serpent would have to eat the dust of the ground. I will come back to a possible interpretation for this description of the serpent later in this book. For now, suffice it to say, this similar reference to the serpent is a key to understanding that both the author of this story in Genesis and the author of Isaiah 65 probably were describing the same situation—one looking to the past and the other looking to the future.

Many theories have been posited regarding the authorship and purpose of Isaiah 56–66, which often is referenced as Third Isaiah. I have no intention of reviewing all of the literary analyses of this remarkable prophetic vision. For the purpose of this inquiry, I accept that Third Isaiah probably was written in the latter half of the sixth century BCE or early part of the fifth century BCE, and portrays God as the one who would rule over Israel and Judah. Following the return from Babylon, the people of Israel and Judah had to decide who would rule the people. In the absence of the monarchy, the disciples of Isaiah were the ones who expressed the hope that Yahweh would reign among the people once again.

According to the authors of Third Isaiah, God was the one who would show mercy on the people for their past iniquity (Isa 60:10) and heal those who had turned away (57:18–19). In gathering the outcasts of Israel (56:8), God would renew a covenant with the people (59:21) and bring them to the holy mountain (56:7) where God would reign forevermore. As their Savior, Redeemer (59:20), and Everlasting Light (60:19), the glory of God would rise upon the people (60:1) and be their guide in the way of righteousness, justice, and peace.

In return, the people were to forsake their former ways of sin, transgression, iniquity, wickedness, and evil. Now that they have been assured by God that they no longer would be abandoned or forsaken (62:4), they were to take refuge in God (57:13), keep the Sabbath (56:2), possess the land (57:13), do justice (56:1), refrain from all violence (60:18), and do nothing that would result in the devastation or destruction within their borders (60:18). In doing all that God has asked of them, they would inherit the holy mountain (57:13) where God would reign forevermore as the one who declares, "Here I am (58:9)."

Throughout these eleven chapters of Isaiah, there is no specific indication by these disciples of Isaiah that the monarchy is to be reinstated in order to galvanize and lead the people into the future. The only reference to the kings of Israel and Judah is in a negative comment about the shepherds (kings) who have turned away from God (56:11). Otherwise, as the people engage in the challenge of resettling in a land that has been laid waste by years of conquest and neglect, God is presented in Third Isaiah as the one who would reign over the land from the holy mountain of Jerusalem forevermore.

In this context, God is portrayed as the one who would create new heavens and a new earth. Everything from the past—all sins, transgressions and iniquities—would be forgotten. Jerusalem would be re-established as a joy and delight for the people. No more would the sound of weeping or the cry of distress be heard in Jerusalem, as was the case prior to the conquest by the Babylonians. Under the reign of God, the premature or unnecessary death of infants due to child sacrifice, poverty, injustice, or warfare would be no more. Everyone would be able to live to a ripe old age.

In this new creation described in Third Isaiah, no longer would some people be forced to build houses for other people to inhabit or be required to plant vineyards that would be harvested by slaves in order to put food on the landowner's table. This description is a reference that hearkens back to the practice under the monarchy when people would become indebted to wealthy landowners and be forced by the authority of the king to serve as slaves to the landowners until the debt was paid off. In the process, the slaves, which included entire families, lost ownership of all of their property. They no longer had anything of importance that they could call their own.

The new heavens and new earth that God would create would restore the policy throughout the land that everyone would build their own houses and inhabit them, and everyone would plant vineyards on their own piece of property and eat from their own gardens. Under these conditions, everyone would be able to enjoy the work of their own hands. No longer would people have to work in vain as slaves for someone else's profit. Most importantly, given the severe conditions of slavery under the monarchy that often resulted in the premature death of infants, in this new creation, women no longer had to live in terror of bearing children for calamity.

Given all that was to be established by God in this new creation, peace would reign throughout the land. This peace is best portrayed in the author's description of the wolf and lamb feeding together and the lion eating straw like the ox. Under God's reign, no one would hurt another or destroy what belongs to another in all of God's holy mountain. Only the serpent would continue to eat the dust of the ground.

This reference to the serpent is Third Isaiah's strongest link to the pronouncements by God in Gen 3:14–19 where God declares to the serpent, "Cursed are you among all animals and among all wild creatures; upon your belly you shall go, and dust you shall eat all the days of your life." In the context of Third Isaiah, we hardly have a clue as to whom or what this serpent refers. For this reason, the reference to the serpent in the story of Eve and Adam becomes critical in understanding the reference to the serpent in Third Isaiah—a point that will be addressed later in this book.

As a result of this direct connection between Isa 65:17–25 and Gen 3:14–19, the description of the new creation in Isa 65:17–25 provides some new insight into the meaning of God's pronouncement to the woman and the man in the story of Eve and Adam. Whereas the pain mentioned in Gen 3:16 most often is explained as the physical pain associated with giving birth, the author of Third Isaiah indicates that the pain associated with giving birth has to do with the anticipated brevity of life. I can hardly imagine the pain that a woman must feel if she knows that she is going to give birth to a child for this kind of calamity. In Isaiah 65, this calamity probably refers to the anticipated brevity of a child's life due to the political and economic environment into which the child is born. Perhaps this same situation is the cause of pain for the woman in Gen 3:16. If so, then who is responsible for creating this calamity in the first place or creating an environment where infants and children would face certain premature death?

Similarly, the labor of the man mentioned in Gen 3:17 most often is explained as the effort that every man throughout history must give in order to put food on his table for himself and his family. However, this universal application for the purpose of work is challenged by the description in Isaiah 65 regarding the slave labor that was established and enforced by the monarchy. If the idea of slave labor also is applied to Gen 3:17–19, then this description in Genesis takes on a whole new meaning. Rather than some universal pronouncement about men who have to work so hard to put food on their table, could God be speaking about the conditions of slavery that were the result of those in power who forced their own people to labor in the fields so that they could enjoy their luxurious lifestyles? Given the harsh realities of slavery, death always was an imminent possibility.

Although there is no clear parallel in Isa 65:17–25 to the reference in Gen 3:16 about the husband ruling over the woman while she still has a desire for her husband, the other similarities between these two texts suggest that this statement in Gen 3:16 also is a critique of what took place under the monarchy regarding the status of women in society. The intensification of the patriarchal system during this monarchical period even spilled over into the relationship between a husband and a wife. The inclusion of this statement in Gen 3:16 suggests that the relationships between men and women, and particularly between husbands and wives, were different prior to the establishment of the monarchy.

For those who assume that the story of Eve and Adam was written much earlier during the time of the monarchy, this description of the new creation in Isa 65:17–25 is viewed as a corrective to the disobedience of Eve and Adam as described in Genesis 3. For example, Brueggemann asserts that this poem has its eye on the terrible verdicts of Genesis 3 and offers the possibility of a new world in which God will right all wrongs described in Genesis 3. In this new world, there will be no more cry of grief associated with death, no more infant mortality, no more usurpation of property and displacement from home, no more absence of God from the face of the earth, no more fracture of creation by hostility, and no more hurting or destroying on the earth.[1] Although Brueggemann makes the connection between Isaiah 65 and Genesis 3, he offers no indication for the dating of Genesis 3 in this writing and leaves the reader with the impression that Genesis 3 was a much earlier rendition of Isaiah's imagination of a new creation that offers a reversal for what happened in the beginning of time.

Douglas Jones makes a similar connection between Isaiah 65 and Genesis 3. Given the reference to the serpent in Isa 65:25, the prophet is demonstrating that the new creation of the messianic age will involve the restoration of the conditions that were present in the beginning when God originally created the heavens and the earth. The one exception to this restoration will affect the serpent which will have to be content with the food appointed for it by God's primeval decision.[2] George Knight also hearkens back to the two creation accounts in Genesis 1–3 by stating that this prophecy in Isaiah is describing God's continuing creative love that will create new heavens and a new earth, and bring good out of evil by restoring the Garden of Eden to its original state. Third Isaiah presents this vision of a future that is eternally present due to God's continuous redeeming love. In this new creation, every child will live to be a hundred years old without a life of tragedy or pain, and every person will experience the joy of a fulfilled vocation by discovering that ordinary daily life has some ultimate significance. Gone are the days when children will die

---

1. Brueggemann, *Texts Under Construction*, 45–46.
2. Jones, *Isaiah 56–66*, 111–14.

in their infancy and when people will have no satisfaction in their daily labor.³

If the vision of Isa 65:17–25 is a corrective to the disobedience of Eve and Adam in Genesis 3, I began to wonder why the author of Third Isaiah, and particularly of this vision of new heavens and a new earth, doesn't make any specific reference to Eve or Adam or to the Garden of Eden. With this question in mind, I entertained the possibility that the similarity of references to the serpent in these two accounts would suggest that they could have been written during the same time period—one as a critique of the past from the perspective of being deported and one as a vision for the future from the perspective of what could be under a different form of governance, but both acknowledging that the former monarchy would not be a contributing influence in the future peace of Gods' reign on earth.

Before I could proceed any further with this inquiry, I decided to review some of the traditional perspectives about the authorship and date of this story of Eve and Adam. From my earliest studies of Genesis, I was taught that the author of this story in Genesis traditionally was identified as the Yahwist because the author uses the name of Yahweh for God.⁴ Who this Yahwist was remains a mystery. Given the evidence of this reference to Yahweh throughout the Hebrew Scriptures, the date when this Yahwist wrote this story also remains in question. In fact, this Yahwist could be one person or several persons who wrote this story at a certain time in history, or could include several authors and editors spread over several centuries of history.

Whereas Meyers argues that Genesis 2–3 generally is considered part of the oldest tradition of the Hebrew Scriptures because these chapters are reflective of the harsh life in agrarian Palestine prior to the monarchy,⁵ Gowan argues for a pre-monarchical date for this story because there is no reference to any kings in this account.⁶ Contrary to this point of view, Coote claims that the Yahwist's account of this story could not have been composed earlier or later than the united monarchy of David and Solomon because this account reflects no concept of a divided kingdom

---

3. Knight, *The New Israel*, 96–100.
4. Fretheim, *Creation*, 67.
5. Meyers, "Gender Roles," 137.
6. Gowan, *From Eden to Babel*, 34–36.

and is written to endorse and support the ruling house of David. Drawing upon various ancient Babylonian creation accounts of the Enuma Elish and Gilgamish epics, the Yahwist has reformulated them in the secular and urban context of Jerusalem which had become the political center for Israel.[7] Fretheim agrees with Coote and specifically dates the authorship of this story during the period of the united monarchy of Israel (1020–921 BCE).[8]

Although stating that the dating of this story is questionable, Werner Schmidt suggests that the Yahwist probably wrote this story during the reign of Solomon and refutes a later authorship of this account because it has no reference to the literary characteristics of the prophets, to the great threat of Assyria, to the centralization of the cult under Josiah (621 BCE), or to the destruction of the temple in Jerusalem (587 BCE).[9] Ellis is much more definite in his assessment of the Yahwist and claims that this story was written during the reign of Solomon when the mythology of Canaan and Mesopotamia had a strong influence on the religious life of Israel in order to explain why Israel is suffering at this time.[10] Although he claims that the origins of Genesis 2–3 are mere guesswork, L'Heureaux argues that this account serves as a critique of a king who refuses to accept the limits that God placed on his authority and decides to be like God in ruling over the people.[11]

Anne Gardner deduces that this story was written during the later monarchical period and describes how God placed the chosen people in the land of Israel, a land flowing with milk and honey. However, as the people continued to demonstrate their disobedience and disloyalty to Yahweh, eventually they could be ejected from the land that they had been given by God, just as Eve and Adam had been sent out of the garden.[12] Although not specifying the exact time when this story was written, William Brown argues that this story could not have been written during the reign of David and Solomon, but suggests a later date during the monarchy in order to remind the people of their roots in the garden

---

7. Coote, *The Bible's First History*, 300.
8. Fretheim, *Creation*, 13.
9. Schmidt, "A Theologian," 68.
10. Ellis, *The Yahwist*, 57–61.
11. L'Heureaux, *In and Out of Paradise*, 61.
12. Gardner, "Genesis 2:4b–3," 15–16.

and warn any king who forgets this blessing.[13] Given the lack of consensus about the date when this story of Eve and Adam was written, I began to lean toward the likelihood that the author of the story of Eve and Adam might be a contemporary of the author of Third Isaiah.

13. Brown, *The Ethos of the Cosmos*, 218.

3

The Lens of Conquest and Deportation

ONCE I REALIZED THAT there was no definitive date for this story of Eve and Adam upon which scholars could agree, I became more intrigued by the possibility that this story may have originated after the deportation of people to Babylon (expulsion from the garden). This perspective was supported by scholars such as Brueggemann who claimed that the exile emerged as the decisive reference point that helped to shape the self-understanding of Judaism. He states that this critical event in the life of Israel and Judah was a time that gave cause for the people to pause and engage in some very profound moral and theological reflection that not only helped the people to understand the failures of their past, but also gave rise to a remarkable production of fresh theological literature to guide them into the future. As far as Brueggemann is concerned, "the exile became the matrix in which the canonical shape of the Old Testament faith is formed and evoked."[1]

Rainer Albertz also concludes that as a defining moment in the development of Israel and Judah's faith and practice, the conquest by the Babylonians and subsequent deportation to Babylon inspired a tremendous amount of theological literature in order to interpret this crisis for posterity. Those who had been conquered by the Babylonians wanted their descendents to have an idea how to mitigate against such devastating events in the future.[2] For those who were deported to Babylon, everything was lost—their land, the temple, the monarchy, the state, and, as far as the people were concerned, God whom they knew as Yahweh. For those who were allowed to stay in Judah, the experience was no less

---

1. Brueggemann, *Old Testament Theology*, 183–85.
2. Albertz, *Israel in Exile*, 139.

traumatic. They continued to farm the land, but they still had to ascertain where they had gone wrong and how they could avert such failure in the future in order to survive as a people.

How might we understand the purpose of the story of Eve and Adam if this story originated during this time of the deportation or thereafter as an attempt to answer this haunting question, "Where did we go wrong?" We can only imagine how this question weighed on the people's minds and hearts as they were forced by the Babylonians to march through the desert to a foreign land where they would be allowed to establish themselves in a new community far away from home. Given this context, I searched through the literature and discovered that I was not the only one who has considered the possibility that this story of Eve and Adam had been written by the Yahwist during this post-monarchical period.

As I summarized earlier, the perspective that this story of Eve and Adam had been written prior to the downfall of Judah has been supported by many scholars in the past. However, this perspective has come under scrutiny by George Mendenhall who suggests that the narrative of Genesis 3 reflects some of the enormous ferment of thought and creativity that resulted from the destruction of the temple in 587 BCE when people had the opportunity to reflect upon this experience and ask the basic question, "What happened and why?" Drawing upon the wisdom tradition of ancient Israel, he concludes that Genesis 3 was written during this period when the people of Judah were forced to live in Babylon as a way to explain the reason for the destruction of their community and virtually all of Judah's institutions as the people had known them during the time of the monarchy.[3] Philip Davies and John Rogerson elaborated on this idea by claiming that most of the biblical literature was composed during and after the exile, including the creation stories which were written during this time period because they bear such close resemblance to the stories and themes of Babylonian mythology with which the people had become familiar during their time in Babylon.[4]

Gary Anderson is very specific in suggesting that the lives of Eve and Adam are retold against the backdrop of the expulsion from the land as a punishment for the people's disobedience of God's commandments.[5]

---

3. Mendalhall, "Shady Side of Wisdom," 320–30.
4. Davies and Rogerson, *Old Testament World*, 109.
5. Anderson, *Genesis of Perfection*, 15–16.

Frederick Winnett specifically states that the Yahwist material originated during the exilic and post-exilic period in order to address a more universal human phenomenon of sin and the apparent consequences.[6] John Van Seters recognizes a direct literary connection between this Genesis account and the Babylonian myth of Marduk, and concludes that the Yahwist has written this story as a commentary on the Deuteronomistic covenant tradition based upon the experience of the exile.[7] Stordalen argues that since the Deuteronomistic History probably was written during the exilic period, the story of Eve and Adam would have to be written subsequent to the popularization of this historical account.[8]

From a different perspective, another argument for the later composition of this story is offered by Bellis who states that the story of Eve and Adam is not mentioned by any of the later authors in the Hebrew Bible. Only in the second century BCE did this story start to be referenced and used by authors of other biblical material.[9] Bloom and Rosenberg support this rationale by stating that no prophet, no chronicler, and no poet in the rest of the Hebrew Bible ever comments about what Yahweh did in the Garden of Eden or what Eve and Adam did to warrant expulsion from the garden.[10] Had this important story been circulating or written down much earlier in the history of Israel and Judah, certainly someone would have made mention of Yahweh's formation of Eve and Adam prior to the conquest and deportation by the Babylonians.

Now that I realized that there was a distinct possibility that this story of Eve and Adam had been written during the time after the people had returned from Babylon, I began to explore who in the Yahwist tradition might have authored this story. As I examined what transpired during this period from the time that the people of Judah were deported to Babylon until the time that their descendents returned to their homeland, I discovered that there was so little information written down about what happened during this time, either in Babylon or in Judah, that much of that experience has had to be reconstructed by scholars. In the course of this research, I learned that for everyone who writes about this period

---

6. Winnett, "Re-examining the Foundations," 1–5.
7. Van Seters, *Prologue to History*, 124–29.
8. Stordalen, *Echoes of Eden*, 207–9.
9. Bellis, *Helpmates, Harlots and Heroes*, 45–46.
10. Bloom and Rosenberg, *The Book of J*, 185.

with some confidence, someone else casts doubt on the reliability of any historical reconstruction.

Even the traditional term *exile* that is used to identify this period has been called into question. Lester Grabbe argues that the term 'exile' is an ideological word that serves to interpret the historical event of deportation from Judah to other parts of the Babylonian Empire. In those days, deportation was the customary way that conquering nations would disperse the people in order to maintain control over a region or nation.[11] Thomas Thompson refers to this traditional maneuver by a conquering country as population transference. Besides, being deported was much better than being killed. He goes on to say that there is no inherent biblical narrative about what happened during the exile which raises the question about the reality of this event in Judah's history.[12]

In my search for information about this time period, I ventured upon a book by Rainer Albertz, entitled *Israel in Exile: The History and Literature of the Sixth Century BCE*. In this book, Albertz reconstructs what may have transpired during the exile and the time after the people returned from Babylon to resituate themselves in their homeland. As a major thesis of his reconstruction, Albertz suggests that four major groups emerged during this period of crises that would lay the groundwork for a new nation in the event that the people would have the opportunity to return home and forge a new beginning. The four groups were:

1. The Deuteronomistic historians who supported a religious renewal with the reinstatement of the monarchy and the restoration of the temple.
2. The disciples of Ezekiel who offered a vision of a priesthood that would administer the temple totally separate from the monarchy.
3. The Deuteronomistic followers of Jeremiah who called for a religious and social reform reflecting the decentralized political structure that existed prior to the monarchy.
4. The Deutero-Isaiah group that offered a vision of a royal theology.

Not only did each of these groups contribute significantly to the literary explosion of this period, each of them also offered a different perspective

---

11. Grabbe, *Leading Captivity*, 18.
12. Thompson, *The Mythic Past*, 217.

about how Yahweh would choose to govern the people in the future in order to preserve the restoration of their nation.[13]

As I pondered these four major groups in terms of which one might have authored the story of Eve and Adam, I easily eliminated the Deuteronomistic historians because they were much more pro-monarchy than this story seems to portray. I also eliminated the priestly writers who were disciples of Ezekiel. Since I already had delved into the theology of Third Isaiah based upon the royal theology of Second Isaiah (Isaiah 40–55), I surmised that Isaiah's vision for the future was a little less pragmatic than the earthy details of this account in Genesis. Consequently, I was left with the theological school of Jeremiah as the most likely source for this metaphorical story about how Israel and Judah were situated in the promised land, how the elders decided to have a king like other nations in lieu of Yahweh being the king of the people, how the oppression, enslavement, and death of the people increased under the monarchy, and how the people of Israel and Judah were deported from their land just as Eve and Adam were expelled from the Garden of Eden.

Comparing what Albertz was presenting in his book with other hypotheses that were being offered about what transpired during these exilic and post-exilic periods, I concluded that Albertz's thesis made the most sense to me. Since no one really knows the facts about this period, I was encouraged by Stordalen's statement that with any reconstruction of someone else's history, all of the facts may not be true, but "for an academic reader, good sense-making ultimately depends upon the ability of a particular interpretation to achieve the stated scholarly aim. It also depends on the relevance and quality of the interest behind the scholarly interpretation."[14]

However, before I could proceed in exploring the possibility that Jeremiah or the followers of Jeremiah had authored this story of Eve and Adam, I decided to review the whole Deuteronomistic History and determine how Jeremiah and his disciples might have utilized some details of this historical account as well as their own experience in this Genesis story. Given that the Deuteronomistic historians most likely wrote their account of the history of Israel and Judah while in Babylon in order to accentuate the worship of Yahweh alone and advocate for the restoration of

13. Albertz, *Israel in Exile*, 134–35.
14. Stordalen, *Echoes of Eden*, 75.

the monarchy and the temple when they returned home, these historians attempted to document over 600 years of history and shape this narrative in a way that reflected the theological message that they wanted their readers to hear. They also crafted a history founded in monotheism and grounded in a temple cult that endorsed a monarchy as the best way to govern the people.[15] According to the perspective of the Deuteronomistic historians, the apostasy of the kings had led to the demise of Israel and Judah. Consequently, the only hope for the restoration of the nation rested in the re-establishment of the idealized monarchy as it had originated with David, without the worship of any foreign gods.

---

15. Lemche, *Israelites in History*, 94.

4

The Lens of the Historians

WE ARE REMINDED BY Albertz that many of the people who were deported to Babylon had been strong supporters of the monarchy and the temple cult. While in Babylon, they were faced with the temptation of worshiping the Babylonian gods that would subvert their worship of Yahweh. The priests, who also had been deported, were creating new ways of worshiping Yahweh in order to keep the people focused on the one God who could save them. In this context, the Deuteronomistic historians were faced with writing a history that would validate and support this emphasis of monotheism and keep the hope of God's gift of the land, the monarchy, and the temple alive in the minds of the people until they returned home. Unlike the prophets, whose critical message about the monarchy was noticeably absent in the narrative by the Deuteronomistic historians, these historians had a high regard for the monarchy and the temple cult that was designed to support this form of governance.[1] I have no intention of reviewing this historical account in its entirety. However, five developments presented by the Deuteronomistic historians are critical toward understanding the historical and political relevance of the story of Eve and Adam.

The *first* consideration directs our attention to what life was like prior to the monarchy. Although the Deuteronomistic historians repeatedly described the land of Israel and Judah as a land flowing with milk and honey, and explained how the leadership of various clans revolved around people known as judges, much more is known today about the environment and relationship of these early settlements. In contrast to the biblical description of fertile pockets of land where water was acces-

---

1. Albertz, *History of Israelite Religion*, 387–90.

sible, the agrarian life in most of the hill country of Palestine was much more challenging than described. In order to deal with the rigor of farming this land, everyone had a significant role to play.

Carol Meyers explains that the main governing units in this environment were the family, and, to a lesser degree, the clan. Living units were relatively the same size—indicative of an egalitarian society. Household units were relatively autonomous. Within this social organization, there was very little social differentiation, and hierarchical differentiation according to gender was minimal. The work to be done was carried out by all members of the family. The roles of men and women were integrally related, with women being involved in all aspects of economic life—in producing, transforming, and allocating resources while bearing more children to augment the work force. Given the important role of women in the welfare and survival of the family, the possibility of any dehumanizing or abusive behavior toward women may have been virtually non-existent.[2]

Marked by a striking decentralization and the lack of any central political authority, families and clans functioned independently of each other and without any external regulation. Economically, the families were largely self-sufficient, and their production was aimed at their own needs. Only when these families and clans were threatened by another political entity did they form a tribal alliance to defend themselves in order to preserve their high degree of freedom and independence.[3] The account of Deborah and Barak (Judges 4) is a good example of the success of such an alliance while Deborah was a judge of Israel.

Secondly, although modern scholarship would suggest that the movement toward a monarchy was a gradual process,[4] the Deuteronomistic historians portrayed this transition at a specific moment in time when the elders came to Samuel and asked Samuel to appoint for them a king like other nations (1 Samuel 8). According to this narrative, Yahweh warned the people through Samuel what would happen if they had a king to rule over them. The king would take their sons to be his soldiers, requisition people to produce food for all of his commanders, and manufacture implements of war for all of his battles. He would take their daughters

2. Meyers, "Women of Early Israel," 36–39.
3. Albertz, *History of Israelite Religion*, 72–76.
4. Cropp, et al., *People of the Covenant*, 238.

to prepare food for all of his courtiers and confiscate the best of their fields and crops to give to his officers and courtiers. The king also would take the best of their animals for his use and food. However, the ultimate sacrifice would come when the king not only would take their male and female slaves to serve his purposes, he also would make slaves out of his own people. Although Samuel was reluctant to grant the elders their wish, Yahweh told Samuel that the people were not rejecting Samuel, but were rejecting Yahweh from being the king of the people.

This transition to a monarchy already was anticipated in the second presentation of the Law (Deut 17:14–19) in which the people were instructed that when they came into the land that Yahweh had given them, they probably would request to have a king like all the nations around them. The king must be chosen by Yahweh and taken from one's own community. The king must not acquire many horses. Nor should the king acquire many wives for himself, or else his heart would turn away from Yahweh. Also, the king must not acquire silver or gold in great quantity for himself. When the king takes the throne, he is to have a copy of the law with him at all times, and read in it all the days of his life, so that he may learn to fear Yahweh. The king is to observe all of the law, neither exalting himself above other members of the community nor turning aside from any of Yahweh's commandments.

For the Deuteronomistic historians who were supposed to be presenting a favorable portrait of the monarchy, this presentation in Deuteronomy 17 and the description in 1 Samuel 8 hardly seem to serve their purpose. However, in acknowledging these common cautions about the monarchy, the Deuteronomistic historians quickly proceeded with their account of the appointment of the first king, Saul. According to Albertz, Saul really provided the transition to the kingship of David, who is portrayed by the historians as the foremost king of Israel and Judah. In order to legitimate this monarchy, David was credited by the historians with the elevation of Yahweh as the God of the nation. Consequently, King David became Yahweh's official guarantor of security and prosperity throughout the land, as well as the administrator of justice and peace.[5] Any wars that David fought were waged in the name of Yahweh and were validated by the royal theologians that David put in office. Although David may be given credit for instituting the transition from the tribal

---

5. Albertz, *History of Israelite Religion*, 116–21.

alliance to a divinely-sanctioned monarchy, Solomon would be most instrumental in institutionalizing the monarchy as it would operate until its dissolution centuries later.

The *third* development by the Deuteronomistic historians that weighed heavily in the historical dimension of the Eve and Adam story was the description about Solomon's dream at Gibeon (1 Kgs 3:1–14). Yahweh appeared in the dream and offered to grant Solomon one wish. Solomon's response portrayed his father, David, as the most faithful and righteous of all kings, and acknowledged that Yahweh appointed him to be the servant king of his people. With these favorable words, Solomon then made his wish, "Give your servant therefore an understanding mind to govern your people, able to discern between good and evil." The Deuteronomistic historians indicated that this request pleased Yahweh, who, in response, granted Solomon's wish as well as giving him riches and honor all of his life.

Although the Deuteronomistic historians identified apostasy as the primary sin of the kings that resulted in the demise of Israel and Judah, they failed to describe how the political and economic policies of the monarchy impacted the daily life of the people. The obvious absence of this information by the Deuteronomistic historians raises questions about their attempt to glorify the monarchy and minimize the social and economic impact that the monarchy had on the people of Israel and Judah. Consequently, the prophets had to fill this void—an omission by the Deuteronomistic historians that contributes to the *fourth* development in the historical interpretation of Genesis 2–3. What the Deuteronomistic historians failed to mention, the prophets exposed and challenged in graphic detail, including in this story of Eve and Adam.

Already under David's rule, the ownership of land that was so precious to every family and clan became subject to royal domination and economic exploitation. Those who had been instrumental in David's military campaigns were rewarded with gifts of land appropriated for state use. However, when Solomon became king, he divided the nation into twelve sections, each of which would supply provisions to the king for one month a year (1 Kgs 4:1–19).[6] He also instituted a royal tax structure to support the royal administration, including the military. For those who

---

6. Cropp, et al., *People of the Covenant*, 260.

could not pay, their land supposedly was confiscated and became part of the royal property that the people worked as wage laborers.[7]

During the prosperous reigns of David and Solomon, some people were able to accumulate wealth while most of the people remained satisfied and situated in farming their own land. However, with the accumulation of wealth, the wealthy landowners were able to purchase more and more land from those who were struggling to make ends meet.[8] Before too long, Israel and Judah's egalitarian society evolved into another situation where a few wealthy landowners owned much of the land while the rest of the people worked as tenant farmers in order to support their families and meet their tax obligations to the monarchy.[9]

This whole situation deteriorated when Solomon conscripted people from Israel to work as laborers in farming the royal land as well as building his palace, the temple, and the fortified cities throughout the land (1 Kgs 5:13).[10] With the increasing disparity between landowners and wage laborers, Solomon's practice of forced slavery gave permission to those engaged in a monopoly of land ownership that they could incorporate domestic slavery as an acceptable means of achieving their own economic ambitions. According to the Deuteronomistic historians, this practice of forced slavery was the predominant issue that led to the resistance by Israel against Solomon and the eventual separation by this northern tribe from the southern tribe of Judah and Solomon's royal authority and control (1 Kgs 11:26—12:19).

With this separation of the tribe of Israel from the tribe of Judah, the *fifth* description by the Deuteronomistic historians that is reflected in the story of Eve and Adam becomes apparent. Whereas once the two dominant tribes of Israel and Judah existed cooperatively side-by-side prior to the monarchy and functioned as compatible tribes under one king, now they were enemies of one another. From this point on in the Deuteronomistic account, the tribe of Israel is portrayed in a very negative light, revealing the bias of the Deuteronomistic historians toward the reign of David within the tribe of Judah.[11] Almost every king of Israel is

---

7. Davies and Rogerson, *Old Testament World*, 37–39.
8. McNutt, *Restructuring the Society*, 159.
9. Cropp, et al., *People of the Covenant*, 291.
10. McBride, "Biblical Literature," 16.
11. Cropp, et al., *People of the Covenant*, 271.

critiqued by the Deuteronomistic historians as doing what was evil in the sight of Yahweh.[12] At one point, they even accuse the kings of Israel as being responsible for the evil that the kings of Judah did in the sight of Yahweh (2 Kgs 16:1–3; 17:19–20). How these five emphases by the Deuteronomistic historians influence the interpretation of the story of Eve and Adam will be addressed in a later chapter.

12. McNutt, *Reconstructing the Society*, 145.

5

The Lens of the Prophets

NOTICEABLY ABSENT FROM THE narrative by the Deuteronomistic historians is any mention of the later prophets of Israel or Judah, or the message that they proclaimed, often in critique of the monarchy. By the time that Solomon had established his reign over Israel and Judah, everything that Yahweh had warned the people through Samuel about the consequences of having a king like other nations already had come true. However, since the Deuteronomistic historians paid very little attention to the social and economic consequences of the monarchy, the words of the prophets have to be consulted and pieced together in order to reconstruct the systemic conditions that existed during the monarchy, both in Israel and in Judah. Whereas the Deuteronomistic historians advocated for a strong worship of Yahweh that served the interests and ambitions of the king, the prophets called for a worship of Yahweh that would serve the justice of the people and secure the peace of Israel and Judah in a manner that existed prior to the establishment of the monarchy.

In their strong critique of the monarchy as the source of injustice and oppression within their society, the prophets would not always mention kings by name, or refer to the king by title. However, when the prophets critiqued the officials, the priests, or the prophets of the royal court, the king usually was the ultimate target of this prophetic affront. Likewise, when the prophets identified those who were wealthy as perpetrators of corruption and violence throughout the land, the people knew that those who were wealthy were able to indulge in their privilege only with the consent of the king. The people understood that the king was obligated to ensure the establishment and administration of justice and peace throughout the land. However, from every example that the prophets named and described that revealed the failure of the king to fulfill his royal duty as Yahweh's servant, the king consistently was exposed as the one responsible for the inequity, injustice, oppression, corruption, and violence throughout the land.[1]

Amos and Hosea were outspoken critics of the monarchy of Israel, the northern tribe. Whereas Amos identified many of the economic and social woes of Israel as evidence of a corrupt and oppressive government, Hosea concluded that the establishment of the monarchy was an erroneous course from the beginning. He insisted that the monarchy was a form of idolatry that must be eliminated by Yahweh if the relationship between Yahweh and Israel was to survive. Hosea, in particular, disclosed that the apostasy that was so evident in Israel began when the people thought that the nation no longer needed to be dependent upon the help of Yahweh alone, but could put its trust in a king who promised political and cultic security in exchange for the people's loyalty and support.[2]

To the south, Micah and Isaiah also advocated for the restoration of Yahweh as the sole God of Judah. In this regard, Micah rejected the cultic practice of his day that allowed for the veneration of the king and proved to be a distraction and cover-up to all of the social injustice and misery throughout his society. Isaiah (Isaiah 1–39) became a prophet when he realized that Yahweh was the king and real ruler of Judah. As a devoted Yahwist who continued to press Judah to worship Yahweh above all other gods, Isaiah denounced the efforts of the people to shun the ethical responsibilities that flowed from their relationship with Yahweh. Both of these prophets were strong critics of the wealthy landowners who had taken possession of most of the fertile land throughout the region. These landowners offered credit to those who needed to survive as tenant farmers and wage laborers, only to enslave the people when they were unable to pay their debts. The luxurious living and hypocritical worship of those who were wealthy constantly were condemned by these prophets, along with their neglect of the poor, the widows, and the orphans in their communities. Justice and righteousness had been forsaken by those whose ambition and greed had allowed them to create such disparity within their society. Yahweh was the only one who could reverse this condition and restore Israel and Judah to the egalitarian nature of their tribes prior to the monarchy. These prophets were very clear. The people must return

1. Eakin, *Religion and Cultures*, 183–85.
2. Albertz, *History of Israelite Religion*, 174.

to the justice and righteousness of Yahweh, or Yahweh would allow Judah to be destroyed by other nations around them.[3]

Although slavery was a manifestation of the capability of some people in society to dominate and control the economic system for their own gain, the prophets were well aware that the current abusive system of slavery hearkened back to the days of Solomon when he forced the people to help build a place of worship for Yahweh and all the other gods of his many wives. As a result of this initiative, the practice of slavery throughout Israel and Judah became more acceptable because slavery benefited the wealthy landowners and maintained a solid economy for the nation. The personal benefits did not go unnoticed, as the landowners would use their slaves to build summer and winter houses for their retreat and relaxation, and tend their vineyards in the countryside so that they could drink their fine wines at home in the city. The treatment of slaves was dependent upon the character of each owner or manager, but the institution of slavery became a normal piece of fabric in a society that continued to subjugate people to the hard labor of working for someone else's profit and pleasure.

Child sacrifice also was a feature of this society that drew the attention and condemnation of the prophets, especially Jeremiah and Ezekiel.[4] To what extent child sacrifice was practiced is debatable, but there are enough references by the prophets to the sacrifice of children, particularly the firstborn, that this practice was of concern to those who viewed it as another example of idolatry.[5] Especially during a time of war when a city was under siege, a child would be sacrificed in order to ward off a threatening army. In this regard, child sacrifice had a royal purpose and became an acceptable part of the cultic religion of the king until this practice was forbidden as part of the reform of Josiah.[6]

Throughout the period of the monarchy, Israel and Judah regularly were at war, either against neighbors of equal status and might, or against the mighty powers of Egypt, Assyria, and eventually Babylon. Although hardly a footnote by the Deuteronomistic historians, the loss of life of young men conscripted into the king's army or the loss of innocent lives

---

3. Ibid., 165–66.
4. Gnuse, *No Other Gods,* 189.
5. Levenson, *The Beloved Son,* 36.
6. Smith, *Early History of God,* 137–38.

of men, women and children during warfare was of grave concern to the prophets, who repeatedly denounced the violence of the monarchy. The prophets also advocated frequently for a more peaceable approach to dealing with an enemy or handling a political conflict.

During the times when Israel or Judah were not at war, the situation and condition in Israel and Judah persisted to favor the wealthy landowners and royal administration over all of the people who had lost their land and were forced to work the land of others, or who worked as servants and slaves of the centralized government and all of the king's courtiers. The prophets, however, cried out most strongly when the king was doing violence to his own people, when judgment at the gate favored those who were rich over those who were poor, when scales were being manipulated to make a profit, when poor people were being bought and sold for next to nothing, or when people were being forced into slavery because they were being outmaneuvered by people who spent every waking hour figuring out how to accumulate more and more land and possessions. The prophets did not always name the infants and children as the victims of these harsh realities, but their fate was assumed in their outcry against the corruption and violence administered by the king and all of his officials and supporters—all done in the name of Yahweh who had been commandeered by the royal priests as the primary God of the monarchy.

Throughout this entire latter period of the monarchy, Josiah stands out as an exceptional king. He reportedly centralized the worship of Yahweh in Jerusalem, cleansed the temple of all worship of other gods, including any sacrifice of children to other gods, destroyed the shrines of other gods situated in the highlands outside Jerusalem, and eliminated most of the cultic practices affiliated with the worship of other gods throughout the land.[7] This worship of Yahweh was not yet a fully-developed monotheism, but Josiah was portrayed as contributing significantly to the movement that would be more fully realized after the conquest by the Babylonians, and become known as the Deuteronomistic reform.[8]

Presumably Josiah did not accomplish this reform on his own. A coalition of supporters for this Deuteronomistic reform galvanized around the discovery of the book of the Law and took it to heart. As a result, Josiah was able to abolish the royal tax, institute the cancellation of debts

---

7. Cropp, *People of the Covenant*, 344.
8. Lemche, *Israelites in History*, 51.

and the release of slaves, make conscription into the king's military more selective, and reduce the size of the military in order to relieve the people of such a financial burden.[9] More importantly, these reformers separated the worship of Yahweh from the people's obligation to the king, and prevented the king from ruling over the people as if he always was acting in Yahweh's stead.[10] Unfortunately, with the early death of Josiah, the theological and social dimensions of his reform soon faded into the past.

Jeremiah, the prophet, played a critical role during this entire time period, from the reign of Josiah to the eventual destruction of Jerusalem by the Babylonians in 587 BCE. According to some of his earlier proclamations, Jeremiah expressed and demonstrated his support for Josiah's reforms. Although he apparently received some resistance from those who opposed the reforms, Jeremiah remained much less outspoken during the remainder of Josiah's reign because the reforms that he favored were being implemented by the king in Jerusalem and throughout the region. However, with the death of Josiah and the ascendancy of Jehoiakim to the throne, Jeremiah was compelled to voice his critique again because Jehoiakim was determined to reverse many of the reforms that Josiah and his supporters had instituted. Jeremiah had to concede that the renewal of the emphasis on worshiping Yahweh as the primary God of Judah had not had enough time to take effect and his reaction was sharp and extreme. Although Jeremiah directed his critique at the officials of the royal court for their apostasy, corruption, and oppression, he also criticized all of the people in society for contributing to the demise of these reforms because they were not able to relinquish the security of their false worship of other gods. As much as Jeremiah is portrayed in the book of Jeremiah as being a lone voice in the wilderness, the rest of the reformers who supported Josiah remained active behind the scenes.

When Jehoiakim sought an alliance with Egypt against the expanding power of Babylon, the Babylonians threatened to destroy Jerusalem. In 597 BCE, Jehoiakim's son, Jehoiachin, who became the king of Judah after the death of his father, surrendered to the Babylonians. As retribution for Jehoiakim's resistance, the Babylonians deported Jehoiachin and a small entourage to Babylon, and appointed Zedekiah as a vassal king, who promised to represent Babylonian interests in Babylon's attempt to invade

---

9. Albertz, *History of Israelite Religion*, 216–19.
10. Ibid., 224–27.

and conquer Egypt. With the appointment of Zedekiah to the throne of Judah by the king of Babylon, the leadership of Judah was divided along party lines—a national religious party that wanted to oppose Babylon, and a reform party, including Jeremiah, that demonstrated a pro-Babylonian attitude. The nationalistic religious party drew upon their interpretation of the prophet Isaiah who had announced that Yahweh would act through a renewed monarchy in order to save the people. If the king really was an agent of Yahweh, then Judah could survive any rebellion against Babylon and remain free. On the other hand, Jeremiah saw the reality of what would happen to the people if the king chose to resist Babylon. Therefore, he proposed that Judah submit to Babylon's rule or incur Yahweh's judgment. With the conquest and destruction of Jerusalem by the Babylonians in 587 BCE, Jeremiah and his few supporters were proven right.[11]

With the defeat of Jerusalem, the Babylonians reportedly deported many of the prominent people of Judah—political leaders, priests, wealthy landowners, and anyone else who was considered to be part of the upper class—to a region near the capitol of the Babylonian Empire. Most of the small-time farmers, wage laborers, slaves, and poor people of Judah were left to tend the land. The Babylonians appointed Gedaliah to be governor of Judah. Given their pro-Babylonian position, Jeremiah and some members of the reform party chose to remain in Judah and seized this opportunity to work with Gedaliah in reestablishing some of the Deuteronomistic social reforms that had been forestalled since the reign of Josiah. Many of the people who owned no land were given the rights to the abandoned estates of the former landowners, including the land controlled by the now-defunct monarchy. New life had been injected into the people, who for centuries had lived under the dominating authority and power of a king. With the leadership of Gedaliah, Judah experienced the reformation of a more egalitarian state—the likes of which had been the custom prior to the establishment of the monarchy. However, this reform was short-lived as Gedaliah was assassinated by a member of the former royal house who could not imagine a community without its king and all of the accompanying royal privileges.[12]

With the deposition of the king and the destruction of the temple, the proclamation of the prophets had been confirmed. Particularly in the

---

11. Ibid., 236–41.
12. Ibid., 241–42.

absence of the monarchy, whether temporary or permanent, the door was opened for various groups not only to fill the void of governance, but also to explain what would be the best course of action for the people in the future.[13] In this spirit of inquiry, the message of the prophets took on a new level of credibility and importance. Once rejected by the majority of the people loyal to the king and the temple cult, the prophetic critique and vision became much more acceptable and influential in the religious, political, and social changes that would be forthcoming.

---

13. Smith, *Religion of the Landless*, 97.

6

The Lens of Deportation and Return

DURING THIS PERIOD WHEN many of the people of Judah were forced to live in Babylon, there were two main groups of people that participated in the interpretation of current events as well as offered suggestions for their future survival: the people deported to Babylon and the people who remained in Judah. Probably the most significant group to consider in this regard was the entourage of Babylonian deportees. Contrary to popular perception, the people who were hauled off into captivity in Babylon were not subjected to slavery for the duration of their stay in Babylon. Although they experienced all of the grief and despair associated with the loss of their land, temple, and loved ones as well as the humiliation and degradation of being forced to cross some 800 miles of arid land in order to be relocated, these deportees were resettled into their own communities where they could run their own businesses and practice their own religion. Most of the deportees were engaged in farming, fishing, or raising livestock. Once they could be trusted, some of them even worked for Babylonian officials, and earned enough to be able to send sizable financial contributions back to Jerusalem.[1] The fact that only a few descendents of the original deportees returned to Judah when they were given this opportunity by the Persians in 538 BCE indicates that the people had made the most of their time in Babylon and had found a way to make a good livelihood, establish a secure home, and experience enough freedom to want to stay.[2]

The tribulation that afflicted these deportees was primarily political, psychological, and religious. Most of the people deported to Babylon were

---

1. Albertz, *History of Israelite Religion*, 373–74.
2. Grabbe, *Leading Captivity*, 149.

religious nationalists who longed for the restoration of the Davidic monarchy upon their return home. For the time being, they held out hope for the continuation of the monarchical rule as long as Jehoiachin remained alive in Babylon. After being imprisoned in Babylon for thirty seven years, Jehoiachin was released by the king of Babylon and dined with the king until the day that he died (2 Kgs 25:27–30). The psychological afflictions were apparent, including the anger and resentment that escalated toward those who remained in Judah and occupied the land that had been left behind by the wealthy landowners. Religiously, the deportees not only had no temple in which to worship, but they also were living in a culture where the Babylonian gods constantly were in their face. They had to decide how they would defend and protect their faith from any assimilation or contamination. In order to preserve and transmit the official religion of Yahweh, the Judaic priests in Babylon established new observances to safeguard the identity and integrity of their religious life. During this time in Babylon, the observance of the Sabbath, the institution of circumcision, the practice of dietary laws, and the emphasis on the family all took on new meaning. During this period, another development in the theology of the people was the official sanction of monotheism as the crux of their faith.[3]

In light of the current threat to this worship of Yahweh by the introduction of so many new gods of the Babylonians, the Deuteronomistic historians, along with the strong proclamation of the Deutero-Isaiah constituency, reconstructed their history to indicate that the worship of Yahweh alone was established long before Israel and Judah ever became organized under a monarchy. These authors, along with everyone else, were fixated on explaining what happened and why these people had to lose everything that had been given to them by Yahweh. For them, the explanation was simple. They had failed to keep the covenant with Yahweh when they started worshiping gods other than Yahweh, when they married foreign wives who introduced foreign gods into their community, and when they went along with their kings who insisted that the worship of a variety of gods subject to Yahweh was legitimate cultic practice. Such a position needed a scapegoat. The logical choice included all of the Canaanite gods which had been a constant threat to their worship of Yahweh, just as all of the Babylonian gods currently were a threat to their

---

3. Albertz, *Israel in Exile*, 102–5.

emphasis on the monotheistic worship of Yahweh. Punctuating the syncretism of Solomon who married foreign wives and introduced their gods to the people, and the apostasy of evil kings like Jeroboam and Manasseh, the Deuteronomistic historians as well as other schools of theology were in agreement that monotheism was the necessary faith of the future in order to warrant the grace and mercy of Yahweh.

One more dominant feature of the theological development during this time in Babylon was the transition from viewing Yahweh as the sole God of Israel and Judah to portraying Yahweh as the God of the universe. With this shift in perspective, the creation theology that was prevalent throughout Babylon became an emphasis in the theology of the prophets and priests who viewed Yahweh as greater than and more powerful than all of the gods of Babylon. Certainly the people of Israel and Judah were well aware of the creation stories of the ancient civilizations long before the conquest of Judah by the Babylonians, but not until they were faced with this threatening rivalry to their faith by such a powerful deluge of religious deities did they have any need to develop their own stories of creation that would present Yahweh as the creator of the cosmos. With the development of Yahweh as the creator of the cosmos came the theological premise that Yahweh was the savior not only of Israel and Judah, but also of the whole universe.

The best witness to this development of creation theology grounded in monotheism was the school of Deutero-Isaiah. According to Brueggemann, creation faith received its fullest articulation in Deutero-Isaiah. Faced with the reality of the Babylonian gods who guaranteed the protection of their empire and victory in battle, Deutero-Isaiah asserted that Yahweh was stronger than the Babylonian gods and had the capacity for liberation in the future.[4] In addition, Deutero-Isaiah provided a revolutionary breakthrough to monotheism by denying the existence of other gods, ridiculing the sanctuaries of idol worship, and speaking of the sole existence of Yahweh who acts alone as the creator of the heavens and the earth.[5] With the imminent deliverance from Babylon, Deutero-Isaiah expected the immediate establishment of Yahweh's kingship within history, rendering a Davidic monarchy superfluous. This theological concept of the kingly rule of God is of decisive significance for the Deutero-Isaiah

---

4. Brueggemann, *Theology of Old Testament*, 149.
5. Gnuse, *No Other Gods*, 207.

group, which proposed the dissolution of the former kingship theology and suggested that Yahweh's kingly rule over Israel and Judah would totally exclude a human kingship bent on the use of political power for political gain.[6]

With the detachment of the religious cult from any royal oversight after the conquest by the Babylonians, the disciples of Ezekiel offered a plan for the reconstruction of the temple in Jerusalem that would be totally separate from any royal palace. The new temple would be consecrated to the glory of Yahweh alone and require no royal legitimization. These disciples did not deny the role of the king completely, as they allowed for a prince to be appointed who would rule with an authority that was significantly reduced by comparison with the monarchy prior to the deportation. However, the priests would claim a new authority that would give them the right to administer the operation of the temple as they desired without interference by a king. In addition to the sacral implications of this plan, the disciples of Ezekiel proposed a comprehensive redistribution of the land in which every tribe had an equal share of the land and every family owned their own piece of land. There would be no more royal requisition of anyone's land, and no taxation of the land that would cause people to go into debt and have to sell their land. The priests also were given plots of land so that they could secure their livelihood from their own labor and not depend upon any royal administration to provide for their sustenance.[7]

Although Jeremiah remained in Judah sometime after the major deportation to Babylon and the assassination of Gedaliah, eventually Jeremiah was deported to Egypt. With his departure, the followers of Jeremiah took the initiative to transcribe and edit his proclamation and make Jeremiah's message relevant to the deportees in Babylon as well as to those who remained in Judah. The purpose of the book of Jeremiah is simple and impressive—that those who read this document will "learn from the mistakes of the past so that they understand the true cause of their distress, and reorient themselves in such a way as to avoid further disaster and really embark on a new beginning."[8]

---

6. Albertz, *Israel in Exile*, 424–25.
7. Ibid,. 427–35.
8. Albertz, *History of Israelite Religion*, 383.

According to Jeremiah, the main reason for the catastrophe of 587 BCE was the apostasy and idolatry of the people that prevented them from a true worship of Yahweh. The threat of syncretism was ever-present—both during the reign of Josiah as well as during the time of their stay in Babylon. As far as Jeremiah was concerned, the only source of salvation was a true worship of Yahweh—neither trusting in the temple cult nor in the institution of the monarchy. Influenced strongly by the people who stayed in Judah after the conquest and who relished their newborn freedom from the oppression of the monarchy and the wealthy landowners, Jeremiah and his followers advocated for a reform from below and an implementation of a social upheaval that would restore a more egalitarian society that was reflected in the memories of the people regarding the life of their ancestors before the monarchy. In fact, Jeremiah was so opposed to the restoration of the monarchy that his followers declared that neither Jehoiachin nor any of his offspring would ever again reign in Judah (Jer 22:24–30).

What transpired in Judah with the return of some of the people from Babylon is as vague as what happened during the period of their stay in Babylon. The primary biblical sources that give insight into this period are the book of Ezra-Nehemiah and the prophetic books of Haggai and Zechariah. Since these books are predominantly theological, the historicity of their content is open to interpretation. However, based upon this information and what is known historically about this period, a general reconstruction of what transpired during this era is helpful in understanding the theological, political, and social emphases and dynamics that emerged.

Many of those who returned from Babylon held unto the hope that the Davidic monarchy and the temple could be restored and rebuilt. One of the returnees was Zerubbabel, grandson of Jehoiachin, who was designated by the Persians to govern the people until he was suddenly removed from office in 517 BCE. With the absence of Zerubbabel, the dream of restoring the Davidic monarchy was gone because there was no one left in the royal lineage to rule over the people. However, the Persians allowed the reconstruction of the temple to continue and it was dedicated in 515 BCE.

In the absence of any formal leadership, Albertz proposes that two groups stepped forward to offer the Persians a coalition that would govern Judah. While in Babylon, the priestly reformers had prepared for the development of a renewed religious cult centered in the temple and administered solely by the priest themselves. With the elimination of any possibility for the restoration of the Davidic monarchy, this priesthood assumed the independence that also gave them a much greater political role in society. The second group consisted of the Deuteronomistic reformers, many of whom had remained in Judah and had been strongly influenced by the prophetic tutelage of Jeremiah. Having been opposed to any restoration of the Davidic monarchy, these elders seized this opportunity to resume implementing the Deuteronomistic social reforms that Josiah had initiated, Gedaliah had reinstated, and a constituency of lay leaders had carried on during the interim. This new coalition of priests and elders was supported by a popular assembly—a model of governance that closely reflected the governance of the tribes of Israel and Judah prior to the monarchy.[9]

Although both of these groups were committed to this social reform, their intentions were tested during the governance of Nehemiah when additional taxation (in addition to the Persian tax) was needed for rebuilding the walls of Jerusalem. Nehemiah chose to force people to be laborers in lieu of paying taxes. The people reacted very strongly to this crisis, especially those who suffered the most because they had to mortgage their fields, vineyards, and houses in order to buy grain for feed and seed, and had to give their children over to slavery in order to pay their taxes. Certainly this social and economic development undermined the egalitarian vision of Ezekiel or Jeremiah's vision of justice for all. However, once the people registered their complaint with Nehemiah, he reversed this policy and imposed a general remission of debt for those who were so obligated. This intervention was simply a short-term solution to a more challenging structural crisis that would repeatedly surface throughout history—the accumulation of wealth by a few people in society at the expense of impoverishment and slavery for the majority of farmers and laborers.

The literary explosion that began with the deportation continued during this time of restoration and reorganization of a society that had been so decimated only eight decades previously. With the failure of the restoration of the monarchy, the Deuteronomistic historians recognized that their aspirations for a Davidic monarchy would probably never be

---

9. Albertz, *Israel in Exile*, 125–31.

fulfilled, but they still could hold on to the hope for a monotheistic devotion to Yahweh which would become the foundation of faith for the religious life of their people. The priests, following the inspiration of Ezekiel, continued to initiate and develop communal laws and rituals that not only would serve the monotheistic emphasis of the people, but also establish the ethnic purity of the community. The prophetic school of Deutero-Isaiah provided the strong affirmation for anything that the priesthood would offer in order to ensure that monotheism remained the focus of the people. The Deuteronomistic disciples of Jeremiah kept everyone aware of the necessary social reforms that must be connected with the monotheistic worship of Yahweh if this theological emphasis was going to serve any legitimate purpose at all.

While all of these documents were being constituted as part of the formal theological foundation for the religious life of the people, this council of priests and elders also set out to formulate the foundational stories that would authenticate the worship of one God, Yahweh, and justify the ownership of the land that became all the more valuable to a people who had experienced both the loss of the land by heavy taxation and imperial acquisition, and eventually by conquest and deportation. There was a common commitment by the priests and the elders to identify the land that would belong to them forever as Yahweh's gift. Neither group favored the institution of the monarchy, but both groups agreed to strive for more solidarity in their society in order to benefit the impoverished farmers and indebted laborers. "Both groups wanted to create a new form of community without its own king under Persian rule, and both wanted a social revolution in order to protect the weak, so they had to reach a compromise over the normative foundation history of Israel if the social experiment was to have any lasting prospects of success."[10]

---

10. Albertz, *History of Israelite Religion*, 481.

7

The Lens of Jeremiah

AFTER ALLOWING ALBERTZ'S DESCRIPTION of these two groups—the priests and elders—to settle in my mind, I thought to myself, "Could it be that these two groups were responsible for writing the first two stories at the beginning of the Hebrew Scriptures?" Drawing upon what I had been taught early in my life about the story of Gen 1:1—2:4a coming out of the priestly tradition, and the story of Gen 2:4b—3:24 coming out of the Yahwist tradition, I realized that these two groups that Albertz had identified could be the authors of these two stories. At this point, I allowed my imagination to lead the way, and tried to put myself in the shoes of these two groups as they exercised their leadership and took responsibility for the compilation of all of the literature that had been written during the past eight decades.

Certainly both of these groups had wrestled with the same question that most people had in the aftermath of the conquest and deportation by the Babylonians. Where had they gone wrong as a people, and how could they prevent similar devastations in the future? From all of their collective experience, the priests and the elders probably had some definite ideas about how to answer this question. If so, then how could they best communicate these important lessons to their people and their descendents so that they would never again have to experience such oppression, violence, and destruction as they had under the rule of the monarchy and at the hands of the Babylonians? One way to emphasize the importance of their message would be to incorporate their perspective into the genre of a creation story, place this story at the beginning of the literature that they were compiling, and convey to their people that Yahweh had been responsible for establishing the importance of this lesson in the beginning of time.

Of course, both the priests and the Deuteronomistic reformers had their own point to emphasize. Therefore, each of them would write their own story and put them in the order that made the most sense at the time. Given that the creation stories of the Babylonians were fresh on the minds of the priests and these reformers who had lived in Babylon or stayed in communication with their counterparts in Babylon, the decision to use this genre of literature in order to communicate these lessons to their descendents was a logical and wise choice.

At this point in the process, I chose to concentrate on the story of Eve and Adam, and pursue the hypothesis that the disciples of Jeremiah, who presumably represented the Yahwist tradition, were the most likely candidates for the authorship of this illustrious story. In order to validate this idea, I knew that I had to learn more about Jeremiah and his followers as well as about the content of the book in the Hebrew Scriptures that is attributed to Jeremiah. Given that Jeremiah had been such a strong critic of the monarchy and that his followers had advocated for some other form of governance than the monarchy after the return from Babylon, the connection between Jeremiah the prophet, the book of Jeremiah, and the story of Eve and Adam had to be well substantiated.

As was briefly stated in a previous chapter, Jeremiah, the prophet, staked out his claim as a prophet of Yahweh during the reign of Josiah, the king of Judah. He was aware of the oppression and violence for which the previous kings were responsible throughout the land. He knew about the sacrifice of children that was included in the rituals of the cultic religion. Jeremiah also was mindful of the disparity between the wealthy landowners and the laborers of the land who could barely earn a living. However, the sons and daughters throughout the land were the ones who ultimately suffered the most under all of these conditions.

Jeremiah was one of the first prophets to rise up in support of Josiah when Josiah initiated his reform in Judah by eliminating the worship of other gods and changing the economic and social fabric of society in favor of those who were impoverished, stuck in debt, or bound in slavery. The early criticisms by Jeremiah were laid aside in favor of advocating throughout the community for Josiah's reform. However, when Josiah was killed in battle, Jehoiakim took office as the king after a short reign by Josiah's son, Jehoahaz, and reportedly, Jehoiakim did what was evil in the sight of Yahweh. Most of the reforms of Josiah were laid aside and Jehoiakim reverted back to the corruption, oppression, and violence of his predecessors. Once again, most of the sons and daughters of the land suffered, while the wealthy landowners were pleased to have a king who catered to their desire to make a profit and accumulate more wealth, including the acquisition of more and more land. Jeremiah had just cause to critique the monarchy and all of the officials of the royal court, but he extended his critique to all of the people of the land because, according to Jeremiah, everyone had become invested in the political and economic system that had been set up by the corrupt and oppressive kings.

Added to this domestic injustice was the imminent threat by the Babylonians who were trying to deal with this buffer state that was located between their expanding empire and the Egyptians. Jeremiah advised King Zedekiah to form an alliance with the Babylonians in order to protect the lives of their people and preserve the security of Judah. Zedekiah chose otherwise, and the Babylonians eventually defeated Judah, conquered Jerusalem, destroyed the temple, and hauled many of the prominent people of Judah off to Babylon. The loss of innocent lives, especially those of the children, was devastating. Presumably children of families were included among the deportees, but the journey to Babylon was harsh and deadly. For the children who were left behind, especially those who had lost their parents in the war, life in Judah was no easier than in Babylon. However, once appointed by the Babylonians to be governor of Judah, Gedaliah tried to create some order out of this devastation and institute some social and economic reforms that were reflective of previous efforts by Josiah. This reform was short-lived because Gedaliah was assassinated. Shortly thereafter, by all indications, Jeremiah was taken to Egypt (Jer 43:4–7).

During the short period following the siege and conquest of Jerusalem, Jeremiah, like so many others during this time of crisis, tried to make sense out of this devastation and destruction. Jeremiah pointed out that everyone, from the king on down, had forsaken Yahweh as their God and gone after other gods. However, Jeremiah laid the responsibility for this transgression at the feet of the king. From the beginning of the monarchy, the kings were the ones who determined the religious life of the people by designating what gods to worship, in what manner, and for what purpose.

According to Jeremiah, he identified the kings, who presumably knew right from wrong, as the ones who often deceived the people into thinking that everything was alright, when, in fact, the kings themselves were gaining profit unjustly, shedding innocent blood, and practicing oppression and violence. The kings had allowed the bondage of slaves and the slaughter of children to continue while making certain that the people of their royal court and the wealthy landowners who supported their cause reaped the rewards of their loyalty. Yahweh may have been named as the patron God of the people, but the kings exercised their own will while pretending to act in Yahweh's stead. Meanwhile, the people listened to and obeyed the kings because they trusted in the king as the servant of Yahweh. As a result of their devotion, the people forsook Yahweh and lost out on all of the benefits of their bountiful land.

Although Jeremiah was not deported to Babylon, he and his followers presumably remained in contact with the deportees in Babylon. Sometimes Jeremiah is recorded as addressing the people who remained in Judah, and at other times, he appears to be speaking to the people in Babylon. For all that we know, some of his disciples were among the prominent people of Judah who were deported to Babylon. They became familiar with the geography of Babylon. The names of the cities, the regions, and the rivers became a part of their everyday vocabulary. They also were introduced to the wealth of creation stories that abounded throughout this ancient culture. These creation stories informed the Babylonian people about their gods and the rivalry that often was characteristic of a multitude of gods. Certainly the number and variety of these creation stories could persuade people that it might be better to believe in and worship only one god. For those who had been deported to Babylon, as well as for those who remained in Judah, the logical conclusion would be that they must believe in and venerate one God, Yahweh, and hope that their relationship with Yahweh could be restored.

For many of the deportees living in Babylon, the restoration of this relationship with Yahweh depended upon the restoration of the monarchy and the reconstruction of the temple. Their hope rested in the release of Jehoiachin from prison and the eventual return to rebuild the temple. By this time, Jeremiah had been deported to Egypt, and, as far as we know, was dead. However, his disciples, who carried on in his stead, opposed the restoration of the monarchy and urged the people to put their trust in Yahweh without having to go through a king. They knew that the people had not been served well by most of the kings of the monarchy. Consequently, the disciples of Jeremiah advocated for a governance that resembled the more egalitarian society that existed prior to the monarchy.

They eventually had their way and participated in the organization of the elders, who, along with the priests, led the people in the restoration of their society and the reconstruction of the temple.

During this time period, there were several theological schools of thought, as described earlier in this book. Although not everyone may have agreed with the agenda of the Deuteronomistic historians, their literary work certainly was influential in framing for the people the role that foreign gods had played in the destruction of their land by the Babylonians. Nevertheless, the Deuteronomistic historians also paid very little attention to what happened to the people of the land as a result of the policies and practices of the kings, who consistently were being accused by the Deuteronomistic historians of going after other gods and building shrines to worship other gods. The prophets were the ones who had to fill in the details about how these royal policies and practices had affected the people. Among these prophetic voices, the disciples of Jeremiah advocated for the well-being of the people by suggesting that the monarchy should not be reinstated because this form of governance allowed one person to have too much control over everyone else in the nation under the auspices of being Yahweh's servant.

The challenge for these disciples of Jeremiah was how to communicate this message to the people and to their descendants most effectively. Obviously, they were engaged in this literary revolution that was taking place and in documenting as much as they could remember about the words and deeds of Jeremiah, while including in this documentation some of their own thoughts and opinions. However, what else could they do to convince their people and their descendants that the former monarchy should not be restored—a monarchy that had been so detrimental to the people of their land?

Using their prophetic imagination (to use a popular idiom of Walter Brueggemann), these disciples of Jeremiah chose to use the genre of a creation story in order to communicate their primary message. To situate their message in the context of a creation story would convey to the people that this message was of utmost importance. They had learned from the Babylonians that creation stories carry this kind of weight. Although the Babylonians developed their creation stories to explain the world of their gods and the origin of life, the disciples of Jeremiah would use their creation story for a more specific and relevant purpose—to remind the people that the way of a monarchy that pretends to be like God or chooses to act in the stead of God would only result in an increase of infant mortality, greater subjugation of women, the enslavement of their own people, and the eventual expulsion from their land. Under the previous monarchy, the people already had experienced such pain and suffering. They would be wise to refrain from choosing such a government again.

Following the attempt by Nehemiah to tax and enslave the people, there was a certain urgency to tell this story. Also, being in dialogue with other schools of thought, which now included the theological school of Isaiah, the disciples of Jeremiah discovered some common concerns in warning the people about the dangers inherent in any form of monarchy in which the kings lose sight of God while believing that they are acting in God's name. Whereas the followers of Isaiah put this message in the hopeful vision of Yahweh creating new heavens and a new earth, the disciples of Jeremiah chose to communicate their message in a creation story that would forever remind the people of what they already knew too well from their past experience.

When the time finally came for this coalition of priests and elders to begin assembling the formative documents of their people and heritage, they each had the opportunity to write their own creation story and place them at the beginning of the literature that they were compiling. Perhaps there were other creation stories that were circulating at the time of these important decisions, but the priests and elders were in the privileged position of expressing their own perspective and bias by situating their stories at the beginning of their formal documentation. The priests used the genre of a creation story to emphasize the importance of the Sabbath, while the elders, many of whom were from the reforming school of Jeremiah, used the same genre to tell a story that emphasized the importance of selecting a form of governance that would not function like the monarchy of Israel and Judah. Any new form of governance must be faithful to Yahweh by making certain that all children, women, and men in their society would be treated with respect and justice so that no child would have to die prematurely, no woman would have to be dominated by her husband, and no person would have to work and die as a slave for another. Through this story of Eve and Adam, the disciples of Jeremiah expressed their concern for the people of their land by encouraging their descendents to make sure that their trust in Yahweh was not confused with their loyalty to any ruler who chose to behave like a god and who oppressed the people in the name of Yahweh.

8

The Lens of the Book of Jeremiah

WHEN I CAME TO the conclusion that this theological school of Jeremiah could have authored this story of Eve and Adam, I undertook an exercise that made this conclusion all the more convincing for me. I decided to read through the book of Jeremiah as assembled and documented by his disciples, and note every significant word, phrase, image, or concept in the book of Jeremiah that matched what was written in Gen 2:4b—3:24. What I discovered was an amazing similarity of vocabulary and imagery that suggested to me a common theology, if not also a common authorship. Once I had recorded all of these similarities, I rearranged and organized all of my notes from the book of Jeremiah according to the outline of the story of Eve and Adam. By doing so, I discovered that the entire story of Eve and Adam could be read in the book of Jeremiah with one exception. The names of Eve and Adam are never mentioned in the book of Jeremiah.

When I shared this discovery with several people, I was advised that this comparison in English could be dismissed as being coincidental unless the similarity of vocabulary and imagery in both the book of Jeremiah and the story of Eve and Adam could be demonstrated in the Hebrew language. Not being proficient in Hebrew, I took the next best step. I looked up every key word in the story of Eve and Adam in a concordance, noted the Hebrew word from which that English word was translated, and then documented how each Hebrew word was recorded and used in the book of Jeremiah. What follows is a summary of this comparison—a comparison that is necessary in order to support my hypothesis that the disciples of Jeremiah could very likely have been the authors of this story of Eve and Adam.

The format of this comparison includes a section from Gen 2:4b—3:24, and then an examination of most of the key words in each section—words that also are found in the book of Jeremiah. After each key word is a transliteration of the Hebrew word in parentheses, sometimes followed by the number of times that this word is used in the book of Jeremiah. Also, all of the chapters and verses in parentheses in this chapter are references to the book of Jeremiah, not to the story of Eve and Adam in Genesis. Since there is no clarity in the book of Jeremiah as to what material originated with the prophet Jeremiah and what material was written by Jeremiah's disciples, references only will be made to the person of Jeremiah in this comparison with Gen 2:4b—3:24 in order to avoid the complex conjecturing of who was the author of what material in the book of Jeremiah.

THE FORMATION OF THE HUMAN

In the day that the Lord God made the earth and the heavens, when no plant of the field was yet in the earth and no herb of the field had yet sprung up—for the Lord God had not caused it to rain upon the earth, and there was no one to till the ground, but a stream would rise from the earth, and water the whole face of the ground—then the Lord God formed man from the dust of the ground, and breathed into his nostrils the breath of life, and the man became a living being. (Gen 2:4b–7)

The story of Eve and Adam begins "in the day" (*yom*—66 times in Jeremiah). Jeremiah also uses this complete phrase at least twelve times to express when Yahweh is about to act (7:22; 39:17). Jeremiah's reference to God as Yahweh is consistent with the way that God is referenced throughout this story, making Jeremiah as qualified as anyone to be a Yahwist. Jeremiah often uses the verb "make" to portray Yahweh as the one who made ('*aśah*—29 times) the "earth" ('*erets*—48 times) by Yahweh's power (10:12, 27:5; 51:15) and who made the "heavens" (*shamayim*—31 times) and the earth (32:17). Jeremiah also uses these words of heavens and earth in conjunction with each other at least 4 times (23:24; 32:17; 33:25; 51:48). From the outset, Jeremiah makes it clear that Yahweh is the sole creator of the heavens and the earth. The field (*śadah*—24 times) that exists in this story often is mentioned by Jeremiah with phrases like trees of the field (7:20), herb (*'eseb*—1 time) of the field (12:4), and beasts of the field (27:6).

The image that God has not yet caused it to rain (*matar*) on the earth (*'erets*) is paralleled by Jeremiah's image that there was no rain (*geshem*) in the earth (14:4). Of course, the man or human (*'adam*—29 times) is one of the main characters in this story that gets similar attention in Jeremiah. A significant image of tilling (*'abad*—1 time) the earth (*'adamah*—5 times) in this story reflects those who till the land in which they dwell (27:11). Although there is no linguistic parallel to the stream (*'ed*) or the act of watering (*shaqah*) in Jeremiah, he frequently uses the image of water (*mayim*—27 times). A notable parallel to this story is repeated twice in Jeremiah (10:13, 51:16) when he states that there is a tumult of waters (*mayim*) in the heavens (*shemayim*) and Yahweh makes a mist (*nasi*—2 times) to rise (*'alah*—15 times) from the ends of the earth (*'erets*). Four times Jeremiah uses the phrase "face" (*panim*—28 times) of the earth or ground (8:2, 16:4, 25:26, and 28:16).

Another significant verb in this story of Eve and Adam portrays Yahweh as the one who formed (*yatsar*—3 times) the human (*'adam*) from the dust of the ground. In Jeremiah, Yahweh is portrayed as the one who formed Jeremiah in the belly (1:5), formed all things, including Israel and Judah (10:16), and formed the earth (33:2). With this particular use of the verb *to form*, Jeremiah identifies his own manner of origin with that of the origin of the human in this story. The life (*chaiyim*—4 times) that Yahweh breathes into the human's nostrils in order to make the human a living (*chai*—5 times) being (*nephesh*—26 times) is mentioned in Jeremiah with references like "the fountain of living waters" (2:13), "the land of the living" (11:19), "their being shall become like a watered garden" (31:12), and "your life (being) shall be spared" (38:17).

THE GARDEN IS PLANTED

And the Lord God planted a garden in Eden, in the east; and there he put the man whom he had formed. Out of the ground the Lord God made to grow every tree that is pleasant to the sight and good for food, the tree of life also in the midst of the garden, and the tree of the knowledge of good and evil. A river flows out of Eden to water the garden, and from there it divides and becomes four branches. The name of the first is Pishon; it is the one that flows around the whole land of Havilah, where there is gold; and the gold of that land is good, bdellium and onyx stone are there. The name of the second river is Gihon; it is the one that flows around the whole land of Cush. The name of the third river is Tigris, which flows east of Assyria. And the fourth river is the Euphrates. (Gen 2:8-14)

At this point in the story, Yahweh plants (*nata'*—14 times in Jeremiah) a garden (*gan*—3 times) just as Yahweh plants the house of Israel and the house of Judah as a choice vine (2:21) in a pleasant land that is the most beautiful heritage of all the nations (3:19), and in a land flowing with milk and honey (11:5; 32:22). Jeremiah has just described what Eden means—luxury, pleasure, or delight—without ever using the proper name of Eden. Then Yahweh puts (*śum*—4 times) the human in the garden, just as Yahweh would bring the house of Judah and the house of Israel (3:18) into a plentiful land to eat its fruit and its good things (2:7).

Out of this ground (*'adamah*), Yahweh made to grow every tree (*'ets*—8 times) just as those who trust in Yahweh are planted by the water, sending out their roots by the stream (17:8). The trees in the garden are pleasant to the sight and good (*tob*—28 times). The first tree is the tree of life (*chaiyim*). The reference to the tree of the knowledge (*da'ath*—2 times) of good and evil (*ra'*—81 times) strikes a chord with Jeremiah who most often refers to the people of Israel and Judah as being evil (13:10; 32:30-35; 44:1-23). The names (*shem*—52 times) of four rivers (*nahar*—6 times) are mentioned in this story. Although the river is a minor image in Jeremiah, his references to the waters of the Nile (2:18), the country of Assyria (50:17-18), and the river Euphrates (13:4-7; 46:2-10) make a significant connection with this story.

THE COMMAND OF YAHWEH

The Lord God took the man and put him in the garden of Eden to till it and keep it. And the Lord God commanded the man, "You may freely eat of every tree of the garden; but of the tree of the knowledge of good and evil you shall not eat, for in the day that you eat of it you shall die." (Gen 2:15-17)

Then Yahweh placed the human (*'adam*) in the garden to till and keep (*shamar*—4 times) it, just as Jeremiah portrays the people of Israel and Judah being placed in the land and given a law and commandments to keep (16:11; 35:18). This dynamic of Yahweh commanding (*savah*—35 times) the human is a major part of the covenant relationship between

Yahweh and the people of Israel and Judah as described by Jeremiah (7:22–31; 11:1–8). In the story of Eve and Adam, Yahweh allows the human to eat (*'akal*—13 times) of every tree in the garden, except of the tree of the knowledge of good and evil. However, in the day that the human eats of this tree, the human shall die (*muth*—26 times). Similarly, Jeremiah describes how Yahweh tells the people to plant gardens and eat what they produce (29:5), but then warns the people of Israel and Judah that if they do not do as Yahweh commands, they will die (*muth*) as a result of their iniquity (31:30).

THE SEARCH FOR A PARTNER

> *Then the LORD God said, "It is not good that the man should be alone; I will make him a helper as his partner." So out of the ground the LORD God formed every animal of the field and every bird of the air, and brought them to the man to see what he would call them; and whatever the man called every living creature, that was its name. The man gave names to all cattle, and to the birds of the air, and to every animal of the field; but for the man there was not found a helper as his partner. So the LORD God caused a deep sleep to fall upon the man, and he slept; then he took one of his ribs and closed up its place with flesh. And the rib that the LORD God had taken from the man he made into a woman and brought her to the man. Then the man said, "This at last is bone of my bones and flesh of my flesh; this one shall be called Woman, for out of Man this one was taken." Therefore a man leaves his father and his mother and clings to his wife, and they become one flesh. And the man and his wife were both naked, and were not ashamed.* (Gen 2:18–25)

In the next section of this story, the author describes an intricate process of finding a match for the human so that the human would not be alone. The details of such a process are not paralleled in Jeremiah, but the vocabulary of this process is very similar to the language of Jeremiah, who describes how the house of Judah shall join with the house of Israel and together settle in the land that Yahweh gave them (3:18). According to the process described in this story, Yahweh formed (*yaṣar*) every beast (*chaiyah*—3 times) of the field (*śadah*) and every bird (*'oph*—6 times) of the air (*shamayim*), just as Jeremiah references the beasts of the field (27:6; 28:14) and the birds of the heavens (4:25; 9:10; 15:3; 16:4; 19:7). Then Yahweh brought (*bo'*—43 times) them to the human to see (*ra'ah*—46 times) what the human would call (*qara'*—17 times) them. The human gave names (*shem*) to all these creatures, but no companion was found (*matsa*—25 times) for the human. So Yahweh caused a deep sleep to fall (*nehal*—3 times) upon the human and while the human slept (*yashen*—2 times), Yahweh took one of the human's ribs and covered the place with flesh (*basar*—10 times).

The woman (*ishshah*—5 times) that Yahweh made was brought to the human (*'adam*), who then named the woman, and identified himself as a man (*'ish*—54 times). Although there is no parallel description of a man leaving (*'azab*—5 times) his father (*'ab*—14 times) and mother (*'em*—9 times) and clinging (*dabaq*—1 time) to his wife (*ishshah*) in Jeremiah, the imagery is a strong parallel with the description of Israel and Judah prior to the establishment of the monarchy when Yahweh says to the house of Jacob and all the families of the house of Israel, "I remember the devotion of your youth, your love as a bride" (2:2). To be of one flesh is descriptive of the cooperative and collaborative relationship that existed between Israel and Judah prior to the establishment of the monarchy when the house of Judah joined with the house of Israel, and together they settled in the land that Yahweh had promised to their ancestors (3:18).

Although both Eve and Adam (the popular idiom for the man and his wife) were naked, neither of them was ashamed (*bosh*—15 times). Without using the word "naked," Jeremiah does talk about the shame of the house of Israel and the house of Judah that they experience for their abominations (6:15; 8:12) and for having forsaken Yahweh (17:13). Jeremiah also directs this shame to the shepherds (kings) for what they have sown and harvested (12:10-13) and specifically to Jehoiakim for all of his wickedness (22:22). Drought (14:1-4) and conquest (15:9) also will bring shame upon the people because the experience will remind the people of what they have done against Yahweh. As of yet, however, the story of Eve and Adam indicates that there is no need to be ashamed prior to the appearance of the serpent.

THE FRUIT OF THE TREE

Now the serpent was more crafty than any other wild animal that the LORD God had made. He said to the woman, "Did God say, 'You shall not eat from any tree in the garden?'" The woman said to the serpent, "We may eat of the fruit of the trees in the garden;

> but God said, 'You shall not eat of the fruit of the tree that is in the middle of the garden, nor shall you touch it, or you shall die.'" But the serpent said to the woman, "You will not die; for God knows that when you eat of it your eyes will be opened, and you will be like God knowing good and evil." So when the woman saw that the tree was good for food, and that it was a delight to the eyes, and that the tree was to be desired to make one wise, she took of the fruit and ate; and she gave some to her husband, who was with her, and he ate. Then the eyes of both were opened, and they knew that they were naked; and they sewed fig leaves together and made loincloths for themselves. (Gen 3:1-7)

The serpent (*nachash*—2 times) is mentioned only twice in Jeremiah (8:17; 46:22), neither of which has any relationship to this story. Although Jeremiah does note how "the heart is devious above all else (17:9)," the craftiness of the serpent is not reflected by Jeremiah. Therefore, the meaning of the serpent in this story, as with the metaphors of Eve and Adam, will have to wait until the rest of the story is put in the context of what the disciples of Jeremiah were attempting to communicate to their people. According to Jeremiah, once the people listened to the voice of their devious hearts, and stood in front of the tree of the knowledge of good and evil, all that they had to do was decide to take a bite of the fruit (*peri*—10 times) and choose to have a king to rule over them. As Jeremiah points out, the people believed that with a king appointed by Yahweh, no evil would come upon them, and they would see neither sword nor famine (5:12).

For Jeremiah, the tree is a vivid image of this stubborn evil will. Kings, officials, priests and prophets say to the tree, "You are my father (2:27)." Israel, the faithless one, went under every green tree, where Judah also went and played the whore (3:6). Under every green tree, the people sprawled out and played the whore (2:20). Judah polluted the land by committing adultery with stone and tree (3:9), while Israel also scattered its favors under every green tree (3:13). In the story of Eve and Adam, all of this temptation is consolidated into one tree, the tree of the knowledge of good and evil.

The imagery of eating (*'akal*) the fruit (*peri*) of the tree (*'ets*) moves from reality to metaphor in Jeremiah. Jeremiah acknowledges that Yahweh has brought Israel and Judah into a plentiful land to enjoy its fruits and good things (2:7). For the person who trusts in Yahweh, that person does not cease to bear fruit (17:8), but all of those whose hearts are deceitful above all things and desperately corrupt, Yahweh will respond accordingly. In particular, Yahweh will bring evil upon the people as the fruit of their devices prevented them from heeding the words of Yahweh (6:19). Whereas Yahweh once called the house of Israel and the house of Judah a green olive tree, fair with goodly fruit, they now have become evil in God's sight because they have burnt incense to Baal (11:16). The person most responsible for this sacrifice of the people is the house of the king of Judah whom Yahweh will punish according to the fruit of his doings (21:14) by burning the trees of the field and the fruit of the ground (7:20).

Was the fruit of this particular tree good or evil? According to Jeremiah, once Yahweh granted the people's wish and gave the people shepherds (kings) of Yahweh's heart who would feed the people with knowledge and understanding (3:15), all would be well. However, such was not the case! Jeremiah concludes that the shepherds are stupid and do not inquire of Yahweh (10:21). They have become gods unto themselves. On any given day, courage shall fail the king and his officials (4:9). Many shepherds are accused of destroying Yahweh's vineyard and making the whole land a desolation (12:10). The king's eyes and heart also are on unjust gain, shedding innocent blood, and practicing oppression and violence (22:17). Basically, all of the rulers have transgressed against Yahweh (2:8).

Jeremiah tries to persuade the kings to have a change of heart, but to no avail. To the king of Judah, Yahweh states, "Act with justice and righteousness, or this house shall become a desolation (22:1-5)." To the house of the king of Judah, Yahweh also declares, "I will punish you according to the fruit of your doing" (21:14). Jeremiah chimes in by expressing woe to the shepherds who destroy and scatter the sheep of Yahweh's pasture and drive them away (23:1-2). Jeremiah also directs his critique of the monarchy at specific kings. Yahweh will treat King Zedekiah like a bad fig (24:8). Zedekiah and his officials also will be punished for their failure to release the Hebrew slaves (34:8-22). Jeremiah also announces judgment against King Jehoiakim, son of Josiah (22:18-19), and against King Jehoiachin, son of Jehoiakim (22:24). He further warns that none of Jehoiachin's offspring shall succeed in sitting on the throne of David and ruling again in Judah (22:30). Given the charge of speaking against the kings of Judah, its princes, its priests, and the people of the land (1:18), Jeremiah proved himself well in fulfilling this calling.

The specific temptation in this story is having one's eyes (*'ayin*—27 times) opened, being like God, and knowing (*yada'*—56 times) good (*tob*) and evil (*ra'*). Likewise, Jeremiah laments that the people have eyes, but do not see (5:21), and the king's eyes and heart are on unjust gain (22:17). As a result of their unfaithfulness, Yahweh's eyes are upon the iniquity of the people, and will bring judgment upon them (16:17–18). In anticipation of this judgment, Jeremiah's eyes will become a fountain of tears (9:1; 13:17; 14:17). Likewise, when the people experience Yahweh's judgment, their eyes will run down with tears (9:18). Eventually, however, Yahweh will set eyes on the people for good and will bring them back to their land (24:6).

Although Yahweh had hoped that the shepherds would feed the people with knowledge and understanding (3:15) so that they would be in close contact with Yahweh after the monarchy was established, nothing would be farther from the truth. According to Jeremiah, under the monarchy, the people do not know (*yada'*) Yahweh (9:3). In fact, they refuse to know (*yada'*) Yahweh (9:6). They do not know (*yada'*) the ordinances of Yahweh (8:7). The people of Yahweh are foolish because they are skilled in doing evil and do not know (*yada'*) how to do good (4:22). Generally, everyone is stupid and without knowledge (*da'ath*) and there is no breath in them (10:14; 51:17). Both the prophet and the priest ply their trade throughout the land and have no knowledge (14:18). Those who handle the law do not know (*yada'*) Yahweh (2:8). For to know (*da'ath*) Yahweh is to judge the cause of the poor and needy (22:16).

Although there is no match in Jeremiah for what might delight (*ta'avah*) the people or make them wise (*śakal*), Jeremiah does indicate that under the house of the king of Judah the people had abandoned the covenant and worshiped other gods (22:9). The people had gone after other gods, forsaken Yahweh, and not kept the law of God (16:11–12). More specifically, the people stubbornly had followed their own hearts and gone after the Baals (9:14). Yahweh would pronounce evil against the people because of the evil that the house of Judah and the house of Israel have done, provoking Yahweh to anger by making offerings to Baal (11:17). Although Jeremiah states that the apostasies of the people ultimately will convict them (2:19), he implies that these apostasies are in direct correlation with the people's desire to have a king like other nations.

At this point in the story, the woman takes (*laqach*—54 times) of the fruit, gives (*nathan*—62 times) some to her husband (*'ish*), and he eats (*'akal*). The deed is done. Then their eyes were opened as promised, and they knew (*yada'*) that they were naked. As stated previously, Jeremiah does not use the word *naked*. However, the association of being naked with being ashamed already has been established in Gen 2:25. According to Jeremiah, Israel and Judah have much for which they ought to be ashamed. As a result of the lack of knowledge of Yahweh, the house of Israel and the house of Judah have been utterly faithless to Yahweh (3:20; 5:11). They have forsaken the foundation of living waters (17:13) and have behaved worse than their ancestors by following their stubborn evil will (13:10; 16:12). Everyone has followed their own plans and acted according to the stubbornness of their evil will (11:8; 18:12). All the people have rebelled against Yahweh and acted corruptly (2:29; 6:28). When the people entered their land, they defiled it and made Yahweh's heritage an abomination (2:7). They also exchanged their glory for something that does not profit (2:11). Within the royal court, both priests and prophets are ungodly (23:11). From the prophets of Jerusalem, ungodliness has spread throughout the land (23:15). Of all that Yahweh has commanded the people, they have done nothing (32:23).

According to Jeremiah, all who ate of the first fruits were held guilty. Disaster would come upon them (2:3). For the time being, their loin clothes are good for nothing (13:10). The stain of their guilt is still before Yahweh (2:22). As a thief is shamed (*bosheth*) when caught, so shall the house of Israel be shamed (*yabash*), including their kings, officials, priests, and prophets (2:26). The people have devoured all for which their ancestors had labored before the monarchy, including their flocks and herds, their sons and daughters. For some people, they could acknowledge that they must lie down in their shame (*bosheth*) and let their dishonor cover them for having sinned against Yahweh and disobeying the voice of Yahweh (3:24–25). For others, they simply refused (3:3) to be ashamed (*kalam*), or did not know how to blush (8:12). At this point in the story of Eve and Adam, the woman and man sewed fig leaves together and made themselves aprons to cover themselves in order to hide their shame. Thankfully, the woman and the man have fig leaves to cover themselves, because Jeremiah indicates that by the time that Yahweh wanted to gather those in Israel and Judah who had acted shamefully, there were no leaves on the fig tree to use (8:12–13).

THE CONFRONTATION AND EXCUSES

They heard the sound of the LORD God walking in the garden at the time of the evening breeze, and the man and his wife hid themselves from the presence of the LORD God among the trees of the garden. But the LORD God called to the man, and said to him, "Where are you?" He said, "I heard the sound of you in the garden, and I was afraid, because I was naked; and I hid myself." He said, "Who told you that you were naked? Have you eaten from the tree of which I commanded you not to eat?" The man said, "The woman whom you gave to be with me, she gave me fruit from the tree, and I ate." Then the LORD God said to the woman, "What is this that you have done?" The woman said, "The serpent tricked me, and I ate." (Gen 3:8–13)

At this point, this story transitions from seeing to hearing, as the woman and the man heard (*shamea'*—124 times) the sound (*qol*—54 times) of Yahweh as Yahweh was walking in the garden (*gan*) in the cool of the day (*yom*). Jeremiah consistently invites the kings and the people to hear the word of Yahweh (2:4; 7:2; 9:20; 10:1; 17:20; 19:3; 21:11; 22:2; 29:20) so that they will know what will happen to them (6:18) now that they have not hearkened to the word of Yahweh. In the story of Eve and Adam, the woman and the man hid themselves from the presence or face (*panim*) of Yahweh so that they do not need to listen to the word of Yahweh. Although Jeremiah does not use the imagery of hiding, he consistently accuses the people of Israel and Judah of failing to hear what Yahweh has to say to them (5:21; 7:13; 11:10; 13:10; 25:4; 25:7; 29:19; 35:17).

So Yahweh calls to the man and asks "Where are you?" The man responds that he heard the sound (not the word) of Yahweh in the garden, and was afraid (*yare'*—6 times) because he was naked (ashamed). Then the man blames the woman for giving him the fruit to eat, indirectly blaming Yahweh for having given the woman to him. At this point, Yahweh asks the woman what she has done, and she turns around and blames the serpent for having beguiled her.

A similar dynamic of blame, deception, and denial goes on between Yahweh and the people of Israel and Judah according to Jeremiah. Yahweh approaches the people and asks, "Where are your gods that you made for yourselves?" (2:28). "Why do you say, 'We are free; we will come to you no more?'" (2:31). "Who can hide in secret places so that I cannot see them?" (23:24). In denial, the people respond, "Why? What is our iniquity? What is our sin?" (16:10). Then they swear by those who are no gods (5:7). Yahweh replies, "I am bringing you to judgment for saying, 'I have not sinned'" (2:35). Then the people respond, "Why has Yahweh done all these things to us?" (5:19). "Why has Yahweh dealt in this way with this great city?" (22:8). The people simply do not see or are unwilling to admit the error of their ways. They continually return to the fruit of the tree that was a delight to their eyes so that they do not have to hear Yahweh's word and do all that Yahweh has commanded them to do.

Why do the people not see the reality of their situation? According to Jeremiah, the false pen of the scribes has made the law into a lie (8:8). Prophets of the king are prophesying a lying vision and deceit (14:14). The prophets of Jerusalem commit adultery and walk in lies (23:14). They delude the people by saying that all will be well with them and no calamity shall come upon them (23:16–17). Yahweh stands against these prophets who lead the people astray by their lies (23:32) and warns the people that they are trusting in deceptive words to no avail (7:8). Instead, the people learn from the priests and the prophets and hold fast to deceit themselves (8:5), growing strong in the land of falsehood and untruths (9:3). They all deceive their neighbors and no one respects the truth (9:5). Worse yet, the people speak friendly words to their neighbors, but inwardly are planning to lay an ambush (9:8). Conspiracy exists throughout all the people of Judah (11:9).

THE CURSE ON THE SERPENT

> *The LORD God said to the serpent, "Because you have done this, cursed are you among all animals and among all wild creatures; upon your belly you shall go, and dust you shall eat all the days of your life. I will put enmity between you and the woman, and between your offspring and hers; he will strike your head and you will strike his heel."* (Gen 3:14–15)

What is the consequence of all of this apostasy, idolatry, oppression, corruption, and violence of the king? According to the story of Eve and Adam, Yahweh cursed (*'arar*—6 times) the serpent (*nachash*) and informed the serpent that it would crawl on its belly and eat dust all the days (*yamim*—50 times) of its life. An interpretation of this verse will be forthcoming in the next chapter, but without a strong correlation with the serpent and dust in Jeremiah, these images in Genesis have to be explained by other words of Jeremiah. The image of the seed (*zera'*—19 times) is used by Jeremiah primarily in relationship to the seed of Jehoiakim and of Jehoiachin. Jeremiah states that Yahweh will punish Jehoiakim by not allowing any of his seed to sit on the throne of David (36:30). He repeats the same message to Jehoiachin, Jehoiakim's son, by stating that the seed of Jehoiachin shall be cast out of the land and none of his seed shall ever sit on the throne of David and rule over Judah (22:28–30). Interestingly, in the story of Eve and Adam, the seed of the woman will strike the head (*rosh*—10 times) of the serpent. In more general terms, Jeremiah also states that Yahweh will reject the seed of Israel for all that they have done (31:37), and that all of the seed of Judah will be cast out of Yahweh's sight (7:15).

THE CONSEQUENCES FOR THE WOMAN

To the woman he said, "I will greatly increase your pangs in child-bearing; in pain you shall bring forth children, yet your desire shall be for your husband, and he shall rule over you." (Gen 3:16)

Yahweh then speaks to the woman and tells her that her pangs (*issabon*) will be greatly multiplied in giving birth and in pain (*'eseb*) she shall bring forth children (*ben*—159 times). Although Jeremiah does not use these same Hebrew words to describe the pangs and the pain that women experience in giving birth and bringing forth children, he does use other Hebrew words as well as other images for describing the pain and sorrow that Israel and Judah would experience as the result of the decisions and actions of the monarchy. During the reign of Jehoiakim, Jeremiah reflects the pain (*makob*) of his cohort, Baruch, who is weary with groaning and finds no rest (45:3). Then Jeremiah warns Jehoiakim how he will be dragged out of Jerusalem to Lebanon where he will groan with the pain (*chil*) as of a woman in labor (22:23). Once Jeremiah begins to experience objections to his position against Jehoiakim, he reflects upon his own life and asks, "Why did I come forth from the womb to see toil and sorrow (*yagon*), and spend my days in shame?" (20:18). Even before the siege by the Babylonians, Jeremiah declares on behalf of the people that he writhes in pain (*yachal*) at the rumors of war (4:19). Once the siege by the Babylonians has begun, Jeremiah talks about the anguish that has taken hold of the people like the pain (*chil*) of a woman in labor (6:24). He also asks the people, "Will not pangs (*chebel*) take hold of you like a woman in labor?" (13:21). When the people are deported to Babylon, Jeremiah writes to them and explains that their pain (*makob*) is incurable because their guilt is so great and their sins are so numerous (30:15).

Jeremiah's description of what happens and will happen to the children of Israel and Judah provides a strong explanation for why women would feel so much pain in giving birth to their children. Most of Jeremiah's description is a warning about the effects of the conquest by the Babylonians on the children of the city of Jerusalem. However, this slaughter of innocent children is only the culmination of all of the poverty, violence, and death that children have had to endure under the administration of the monarchy for centuries.

Jeremiah reminds the people that they have forsaken Yahweh, made offerings to other gods, filled this place with innocent blood, and gone on burning their children (*ben*) to Baal in high places (7:31; 19:4–5). As a result of their sin, Yahweh will allow Jerusalem to fall by the sword before their enemies. However, before this conquest happens, a famine will plague the city during the siege by the Babylonians. Their sons (*ben*) and daughters shall die and none of them shall be left (11:22–23). Also, with their food supply cut off, the people will be eating the flesh of their sons (*ben*) and daughters (19:9). During this siege, there will be nothing but oppression throughout the city. Violence and destruction will be heard everywhere. Sickness and wounds will affect everyone (6:6–7). During the siege, Jeremiah heard a cry as of a woman in labor, the anguish as of one bringing forth her first child, the cry of daughter Zion gasping for breath, stretching out her hands and crying, "Woe is me. I am fainting before killers" (4:31). Likewise, a sound of wailing will be heard from Zion (9:19).

Concerning the sons (*ben*) and daughters born in this place, and the mothers who bear them and the fathers who beget them in this land, they shall die of deadly diseases, not be lamented or buried, and become like dung on the surface of the ground. The children (*ben*) shall perish by the sword and by famine, and their bodies will become like food for animals (16:3–4; 18:21). A special warning is made to the women whose children will be cut off by death (9:20–21). Parents and children will be dashed together (13:14). The ancient nation from the north shall eat up their harvest and their food, eat up their sons (*ben*) and daughters, their flocks and herds, and their vines and fig trees (5:17). When everything is over, there will be no one left to bury the men, their wives, and their children (14:16). Ultimately, a voice of lamentation and bitter weeping will be heard throughout the land—the weeping of Rachel for her children (*ben*) because they are no more (31:15).

Jeremiah makes no reference to the desire of a woman (*'ishshah*) for her husband (*'ish*). However, Jeremiah indicates that the men of Israel and Judah will be conquered by the people from the north and be scattered over the face of the earth because of their abomination, their adulteries, their neighings, and their lewd harlotries (13:20–27). The men have committed adultery, trooped to the house of harlots, and neighed like lusty stallions after their neighbor's wives (5:8). They have polluted the land by divorcing their wives (*'ishshah*) for harlots, and forcing their wives into the position of having to become another man's wife to rule over her (3:1). Women are portrayed in Jeremiah as the victims of domineering men who take full advantage of their marital relationship and then dispense with their wives when they desire greener pastures.

THE CURSE ON THE GROUND

> And to the man he said, "Because you have listened to the voice of your wife, and have eaten of the tree about which I commanded you, 'You shall not eat of it,' cursed is the ground because of you; in toil you shall eat of it all the days of your life; thorns and thistles it shall bring forth for you; and you shall eat the plants of the field. By the sweat of your face you shall eat bread until you return to the ground; for out of it you were taken, you are dust and to dust you shall return." (Gen 3:17–19)

Then Yahweh speaks to the man (*'adam*) and explains that the ground (*'adamah*) will be cursed (*'arar*) because the man has listened (*shamea'*) to the voice (*qol*) of his wife (*'ishshah*) and eaten (*'akal*) of the tree (*ets*) which Yahweh had commanded (*savah*) him not to eat. However, this decision comes at a price. As a result of this curse (*'arar*), men will have to labor all the days (*yamim*) of their lives (*chaiyim*) in order to have enough bread (*lecham*—8 times) to eat. By this time in the story of Eve and Adam, almost every key word reflects the vocabulary used by Jeremiah.

Two examples of this curse in Jeremiah pertain to the person who does not heed the words of Yahweh's covenant that was made with the ancestors of the people of Judah. Yahweh brought their ancestors into a land flowing with milk and honey and asked them to do one thing—

to obey Yahweh's voice (*qol*). However, the people have not obeyed Yahweh nor inclined their ear to Yahweh, but rather have walked in the stubbornness of their evil hearts. Everyone in the house of Israel and the house of Judah has gone after other gods to serve them. Implicit in this indictment is the responsibility of the kings for bringing Yahweh's curse upon the people (11:1–10). Also, Yahweh curses the person who puts his trust in other men (like the king) and depends on the might of his arm to acquire his wealth and treasures because his heart has turned away from Yahweh and is full of deceit and corruption (17:5–9).

In order for the king to accumulate his wealth, Jeremiah points out that under the monarchy, some men are forced to work the fields and toil as slaves because everyone is greedy for unjust gain (6:13). There will be those who build their houses by unrighteousness and their upper rooms by injustice and who make their neighbors work for nothing and refuse to pay them their wages (22:13). Worse yet, famine will come as a result of the people's iniquities (14:14–16). The people's iniquities will turn away the rain and their sin will deprive them of good harvest (5:24–25). Yahweh will withhold the showers and the spring rains will not come (3:3). The fruitful land has become a desert and the whole land a desolation (4:26–27). The earth becomes waste and void (4:23). The land mourns and every blade of grass has withered (12:4). The people have sown wheat but have reaped thorns (*qots*) and have profited nothing (12:13). The ground will be burned and not be quenched because the people have worshiped other gods (7:16–20). The land also is greatly polluted, because of the people's whoring and wickedness (3:1). The final insult will come when Yahweh will hand their fields over to their conquerors (8:10).

Besides suffering under slavery and struggling to put bread (*lecham*) on the table during the famine, the ultimate threat to the man was warning him that they would return (*shub*—35 times) to the ground (*'adamah*) from which they were taken. According to Jeremiah, this dynamic originated with Israel and Judah's relationship with Yahweh. Once the people had been placed in the land flowing with milk and honey and were granted a king like other nations, the people turned away from Yahweh, pursued other gods, and did what was evil in the sight of God. Jeremiah pleaded with the people to turn from their evil ways (15:7; 18:11; 23:14; 35:15; 36:3, 7) and return to Yahweh (3:1; 3:12; 4:1; 8:4–5: 15:19; 24:7). If they refused, then they would be taken from their land, and return no more (22:10).

THE TREE OF LIFE

> *The man named his wife Eve, because she was the mother of all living. And the LORD God made garments of skins for the man and for his wife, and clothed them. Then the LORD God said, "See, the man has become like one of us, knowing good and evil; and now, he might reach out his hand and take also from the tree of life, and eat, and live forever"—therefore the LORD God sent him forth from the garden of Eden, to till the ground from which he was taken. He drove out the man, and at the east of the garden of Eden he placed the cherubim, and a sword flaming and turning to guard the way to the tree of life.* (Gen 3:20–24)

After the final curse, the man (*'adam*) gives his wife (*'ishshah*) the name (*shem*) of Eve, which means the mother of all living (*chai*). Whereas the common name for the man is derived from the Hebrew word *'adam*, the woman is given a specific name in this story, whereby she is elevated to a role of universal prominence rarely afforded women under the monarchy. Although the imagery of Yahweh clothing the man and his wife is not found in Jeremiah, Jeremiah does hold out the hope that according to Yahweh's compassion and mercy, the people eventually would be returned by Yahweh to their land, where they would plant and harvest once again (30:10; 31:8; 46:27).

Until that day, the people would not turn from their evil (*ra'*) ways, but continued to serve their king who usually did more evil than good (*tob*) in the sight of Yahweh. Therefore, Yahweh decided to remove the people from their land and send them to a foreign land where Jeremiah informed them that they should build houses and live in them (29:5), and plant (*natar*) gardens (*gannah*) and eat (*'akal*) their fruit (*peri*). Thus, Yahweh sends (*shalach*—10 times) the man (*'adam*) from the garden (*gan*) to go elsewhere to till (*'abad*) the ground (*'adamah*). After Yahweh drove the man out, Yahweh placed the cherubim with a flaming sword (*cherub*—69 times) to guard (*shamar*—4 times) the way (*derek*—46 times) to the tree (*'ets*) of life (*chaiyim*).

The image of the sword in Jeremiah tells the story of how Babylon would destroy Judah and drive the people from their land. The enemy would come with a sword (*cherub*) and terrorize the people on every side (6:25). The enemy would come and devour the land and all that fills it (8:16). They would destroy with their sword the fortified cities in which the people have put their trust (5:17). They would not act alone. The sword of Yahweh also would devour the land from one end to another (12:12). All Judah would be taken into exile (13:19) and the people would be hauled out of the land (16:13). While in exile, the people would not let the prophets and diviners among them deceive them as they did under the monarchy (29:8). Yahweh would scatter the people among the nations and would send the sword after them until they were consumed (9:16).

Yahweh also would remove the city from Yahweh's sight because of all of the evil (*ra'*) of the people of Israel and the people of Judah, including their kings, officials, priests, and prophets, and all the inhabitants of Jerusalem (32:31–32). Death would be preferred to life by all of the remnant that remains of this evil family in all the places where Yahweh would drive them (8:3). As a result of everything that has happened, the people would know what they had done and know (*yada'*) and see (*ra'ah*) that it was evil and bitter to forsake Yahweh (2:19, 23).

Jeremiah concludes this story with a word of hope. When Yahweh brings the people back, Yahweh will raise up shepherds over them who would shepherd them. However, Yahweh will raise up for David a righteous branch whose name will be called: Yahweh is my righteousness (23:4–6). Yahweh will be the king of the nation, and there will be no one like Yahweh (10:7). Yahweh will renew the covenant with the house of Israel and the house of Judah and everyone will know (*yada'*) Yahweh, from the least to the greatest (31:31–34). If the people will amend their ways, act justly with one another, do not oppress the alien, the orphan, and the widow, do not shed innocent blood, and do not go after other gods to their own hurt, then Yahweh will dwell again with them in the land that Yahweh gave of old to their ancestors (7:5–7). Then life, like the tree (*'ets*) of life (*chaiyim*) in the story, shall become like a watered garden (*gan*) once again (31:12). The gods who did not make (*'asah*) the heavens (*shamayim*) and the earth (*'erets*) shall perish from the earth and from under the heavens (10:11). At some future time, all nations shall no longer stubbornly follow their own evil will (3:17).

This comparison of the vocabulary and imagery between the book of Jeremiah and the story of Eve and Adam demonstrates that there are enough similarities between these two documents to warrant the assertion that the story of Eve and Adam could have been written by the theological school of Jeremiah. The entire story of Eve and Adam can be told from the book of Jeremiah. However, Eve and Adam are not mentioned by name in the book of Jeremiah. Although the absence of their names may raise some questions about this assertion of similar authorship, the questions are answered if Eve and Adam are understood to be metaphors for Israel and Judah, both of which consistently are named throughout the book of Jeremiah.

In this regard, Jeremiah lived and prophesied long after Israel was conquered by the Assyrians. However, he still makes regular reference to Israel as well as to Judah throughout his writings. From the prophet's perspective, the historical memory of how these two nations were aligned with each other before the establishment of the monarchy remains a vision of hope for the future, even with the dissolution of the nation of Israel. At the same time, Jeremiah is fully aware of how both of these nations had suffered the same fate under the monarchy. In order to support his critique of the monarchy, Jeremiah repeatedly would draw upon the experience of both the house of Israel and the house of Judah under the monarchy. Especially after the Deuteronomistic historians developed and wrote their account of how the monarchy was established in both Israel and Judah, and stated that the monarchy was worthy of being restored when the people returned from Babylon, the disciples of Jeremiah had no other choice but to follow Jeremiah's lead and reference both Israel and Judah throughout this book in order to emphasize the fact that neither country fared too well under the monarchy.

Once the genre of a creation story was chosen in which to state their position, the disciples of Jeremiah drew upon their own prophetic imagination in order to convey an important message to their posterity—to be very cautious about ever reinstating a monarchy that would assume to act in God's stead and make decisions that would result in the premature deaths of children, the subjugation of women, and the enslavement of their own people. Israel and Judah had been so closely aligned with one another prior to the establishment of the monarchy that, at times, they functioned as if they were one people. The metaphor of Eve and Adam in this story was a perfect choice to portray this relationship, as well as to describe what happened to this relationship and all of their people once the people of Israel and Judah chose to have a king like other nations.

9

The Lenses of History, Politics, and Metaphor

ONCE ALL OF THIS groundwork had been laid for considering a different interpretation of the story of Eve and Adam, I was faced with the challenge of putting together all of the pieces of this puzzle. As I stated previously, given that this story was written with a tremendous amount of prophetic imagination, not every word or detail of this story has to have some meaning. In the spirit of this imagination, what proves to be most important is the motive for writing this story and the message that is being communicated. In summary, the disciples of the prophet Jeremiah wanted to dissuade their people from reinstating a monarchy that would act like Yahweh and rule over the people in a way that would result in the increase of infant mortality, greater subjugation of women, and the enslavement of their own people. To emphasize their point, these disciples of Jeremiah situated this story in the genre of a creation story in order to demonstrate that this message was of utmost importance for the survival of their people and the future peace of their nation.

THE FORMATION OF THE HUMAN

The story of Eve and Adam begins with Yahweh having made the earth and the heavens, reflecting the more universal perspective of Yahweh that had become the norm during the time that the people of Judah had resided in Babylon. From this perspective, Yahweh also is attributed by the disciples of Jeremiah with the power to produce the water to rain upon the earth in order to sustain all of life. As the author of life, Yahweh is portrayed as the one who formed the human just as Yahweh was perceived to be the one who had chosen the tribe of Israel to be in a special relationship with Yahweh and had brought Israel to life. Looking back on their history, these disciples believed that their ancestors were placed by Yahweh in a land which to the east was a lush and fertile land watered by what was known as the Jordan River.[1] Portrayed in this story as the Garden of Eden and described in Jeremiah as the land flowing with milk and honey, this land was a delight to the people in which Yahweh made to grow every tree that was pleasant to the sight and good for food. For these disciples, a tree was the image of what connected the earth with the heavens where they believed Yahweh to reside.[2] Therefore, in this lush and fertile land once occupied by the tribe of Israel, Yahweh was the one who was their source of life as well as their source of knowledge of good and evil.

THE GARDEN IS PLANTED

This land of delight was situated in the heart of the known world that was defined by the rivers that surrounded it. The Tigris River and Euphrates River, with which the people deported to Babylon had become quite familiar, are the better known of the four rivers named in this section of the story. Scholars have tried to identify the location of the Pishon River and the Gihon River. To the best of their ability, they have concluded that these rivers were surnames for the Nile River and another river to the west of Israel.[3] There is no better way to elevate the importance of their own land than for the disciples of Jeremiah to indicate that out of this land flows a river that had watered the other major nations of the known world—Egypt, Assyria, Babylon, and now Persia. However, given how Israel, and eventually Judah, had been such a significant region that had served as a conduit of trade between these major regions of the world and also served as a buffer between them when they were at war with one another, it took little imagination for these disciples to portray the once united nations of Israel and Judah as being a very significant source of life for these great nations.

THE COMMAND OF YAHWEH

Yahweh is then portrayed as the one who makes a covenant with the people of Israel. If the people obey what God commands, they shall continue to live in this Garden of Eden just as the Deuteronomistic historians

---

1. Hiebert, *The Yahwist's Landscape*, 56–57.
2. Gowan, *When Man Becomes God*, 103.
3. Ottosson, "Eden and Land of Promise," 179–80.

repeatedly had portrayed Israel and Judah's covenant with Yahweh. In this story, the only stipulation that is highlighted by the disciples of Jeremiah is the restriction about eating from the tree of the knowledge of good and evil, which will become more significant later in this story when the serpent speaks to Eve. For now, Yahweh warns Israel that if the people eat of this tree, they shall surely die just as Yahweh commanded the people of Israel and Judah to keep God's covenant or they would die.

THE SEARCH FOR A PARTNER

Israel obviously was not alone in this relationship with Yahweh. Judah also was a tribe just to the south of Israel that these disciples portray as being in a covenant relationship with Yahweh. Among all the other tribes and nations of the region that worshiped other gods by other names, Israel and Judah are the two tribes that are portrayed as recognizing Yahweh as the God who had given them this fertile land. These two tribes had co-existed side-by-side prior to the monarchy, and, for the most part, had cooperated in an egalitarian and peaceful partnership in order to survive in the land that had been given to them by Yahweh, signified by the one flesh in the story of Eve and Adam.

The description in this story about the man leaving his father and his mother and clinging to his wife is significant, not as a description of marriage between a man and a woman, but rather as a description of a matriarchal society that may have existed within these two tribes prior to the monarchy. I was given this perspective some twenty years ago when a Hopi woman spoke at an adult forum at Luther Place Memorial Church. As she described her culture, she made a comment that in her matriarchal society, a man leaves his parents and marries his wife. When I heard her words, my mind immediately went to the story of Eve and Adam. The same phrase had been used by the disciples of Jeremiah in this story to describe a society in which women had a much more prominent role.

As stated previously, Carol Meyers has demonstrated that prior to the establishment of the monarchy women were recognized as having a much more egalitarian role within the tribes of Israel and Judah.[4] Whether women actually were the ones who governed the people is a dynamic worthy of exploration. Looking through the lens and experience of the monarchy as well as the destruction of their temple and expulsion

---

4. Meyers, "Women of Early Israel," 38.

from their land, the disciples of Jeremiah may have romanticized what life had been like much earlier in their history. However, given their collective memory of life under the monarchy, they perceived that prior to the monarchy women played a much more significant role in the affairs of society and contributed to the cooperative co-existence between the tribes of Israel and Judah. Consequently, neither Israel nor Judah had any reason to be ashamed, because they were dwelling together in peace (one flesh) as Yahweh had designed.

THE FRUIT OF THE TREE

Once Judah was conquered, the temple was destroyed, and the people were deported to Babylon, Jeremiah and his followers, as with many of their contemporaries, tried to figure out where not only Judah, but also Israel had gone wrong. What was the pivotal point in their history that resulted in this atrocious treatment of their own people as well as the demise of their nations? Looking back over the past 600 years, Jeremiah and his followers concentrated on the time when, according to the Deuteronomistic historians, the elders of Israel and Judah came to Samuel and requested to have a king like other nations to govern the people. When Samuel prayed to Yahweh about the people's request, Yahweh told Samuel that in making this request, the people had rejected Yahweh from being king over the people. Recognizing this major shift in loyalty, Yahweh then warned the people about the consequences that they would experience with an earthly king who would become like a god to the people. However, the people refused to listen to Yahweh. Instead, they listened to their desire to establish a monarchy, which is the serpent that is portrayed in this story and which leads to their downfall as nations. At least five times in the Book of Jeremiah, the people are described as stubbornly following their own evil heart (3:17; 7:24; 13:10; 16:12; 18:12)—a dynamic that the elders already had demonstrated on behalf of the people when they requested to have a king like other nations to rule over them and go out before them and fight their battles.

Despite all of the warnings by Yahweh, the people of Israel and Judah could not resist the temptation to replace Yahweh with a king like other nations, which, as the story of Eve and Adam recounts, would lead to their demise. Therefore, when Eve, and eventually Adam, take the fruit from the tree of the knowledge of good and evil and eat it, this fateful act depicts the time when Israel and Judah agreed to have a king like other nations. At that time, the idea of having a king like other nations to rule over them appeared to be such a good deal because the people assumed that the king would bring delight to their two nations and make them wise unto the ways of peace and prosperity.

At this point in the story, the designation of this tree by the disciples of Jeremiah as the tree of the knowledge of good and evil is a key to understanding their purpose for telling this entire story of Eve and Adam. Using the metaphor of the tree of knowledge of good and evil, the disciples have reminded the people about the description by the Deuteronomistic historians regarding Solomon's request for the ability to discern between good and evil. Regardless of the personal faults of David and Solomon, the historians had glorified these two kings of Israel and Judah—one as a mighty warrior and the other as a ruler who was wiser than any ruler on the face of the earth. As a result of this deification, essentially David and Solomon had become like gods to the people who thought that these kings could do no wrong while they demanded the people's loyalty beyond their devotion to Yahweh.

However, by the time that Solomon reigned over Israel and Judah, much of what Yahweh had warned the people about the ways of the king already had come true. David had built up an army, not only to defend Israel and Judah from other nations, but also to conquer other lands and expand the territory of the nations. When Solomon took over as king of Israel and Judah, he set out to build his palaces, erect the temple, and fortify the cities. In order to do so, he used his wisdom to coerce many of the people into forced labor, particularly the people of Israel. At the same time, the chief officers of Solomon's court began to acquire more and more land in order to support the mighty army of the king and all of the functions of the royal court. Consequently, the people of the land were forced to work their own land in order to support the king, and eventually would be forced to relinquish their land to the wealthy landowners who were loyal supporters of the king.

When Rehoboam, Solomon's son, took the throne, the people of Israel were ready to rebel against the king because they were the ones who had suffered the most under the yoke of slavery. Instead of making their load lighter, Rehoboam actually increased the burden of the people of Israel. As a result of this bondage, Jeroboam rose up as a leader in Israel and led a revolt against Judah that severed the ties between these two nations for centuries. Both Rehoboam and Jeroboam were assessed by the Deuteronomistic historians as having done what was evil in the sight of Yahweh. However, Solomon's decision to force his own people into slavery was the primary cause for the division that developed between Israel and Judah so that they no longer would be considered of one flesh. Although the people recognized the error of their ways in having chosen a king like other nations and felt the naked shame for their decision, once the monarchy was in place in both Israel and Judah, there was nothing that they could do to reverse the negative impact of the monarchy on the people.

Jeremiah talks openly about the shame that the people have experienced as a result of living with a monarchy that consistently does what is evil in the sight of Yahweh. This shame is depicted in the story of Eve and Adam by the nakedness that became evident to Eve and Adam after they had eaten the fruit from the tree of the knowledge of good and evil. However, as Jeremiah points out, the kings, as well as the officials, priests, and prophets of the royal court, go to great lengths to try to cover up this shame. All of the deception that is conceived by the prophets and the priests of the royal court is summarized by Jeremiah in his critique that they have proclaimed peace throughout the land when there is no peace. They were so successful in covering up all of the abominations that were happening under the monarchy that the people knew no shame, and did not even know how to blush (Jer 6:14–15).

THE CONFRONTATION AND EXCUSES

However, Yahweh is portrayed in this story as being relentless in a gentle way. Yahweh comes looking for the people of Israel and Judah in order to ascertain if they will recognize and admit how they have switched their loyalties from Yahweh to serve the king as their god. In this story, Eve and Adam are quick to make excuses for their disobedience to Yahweh just as Jeremiah describes how the people in his day consistently denied any wrongdoing by asking, "What is our iniquity? What is our sin?" They even blamed God for all that has happened to them by asking, "Why has Yahweh done all these things to us?"

According to Jeremiah, the people who have been challenged by the prophets with the word of Yahweh and warned about the consequences that will come their way if they refuse to repent and return to Yahweh as their shepherd have a tendency to deceive themselves just as Eve and Adam deceived themselves. The people don't understand why Yahweh would threaten to do evil against them if they have been faithful to the kings whom God has appointed to rule over them. However, no matter how many people have turned away from Yahweh and participated in the corruption and violence of the monarchy, the king always is the one who ultimately is held responsible by the prophets for having done what was evil in the sight of Yahweh.

THE CURSE ON THE SERPENT

In order to depict how the monarchy ultimately was to blame for what happened to the people of Israel and Judah, the disciples of Jeremiah indicate in this story that the serpent, as a metaphor for the monarchy, would be relegated to crawling on its belly and eating dust for the rest of its existence. According to Brueggemann, "to cause to eat dust" was the language of the prophets to indicate how Yahweh would subjugate the opponents of Yahweh to nothingness without identity or importance.[5] In this case, the opponent of Yahweh was the monarchy itself which would prove to be of absolutely no value in serving the people whom they were anointed by Yahweh to rule. In fact, the monarchy is the primary cause for all of the pain and suffering that had come upon the people during the reign of the monarchy, and the best way to depict this worthlessness is by stating that this serpent would eat dust for the rest of its existence. Basically, the disciples of Jeremiah have portrayed Yahweh in this story as the one who has declared that the monarchy would no longer have an identity of its own among the people nor have any important role to play in the future governance of the people by referring to the serpent (monarchy) as eating dust forever.

Jeremiah and his disciples had made it very clear that the seed of Jehoiakim and Jehoiachin would never sit on the throne of David. To emphasize this point in the story of Eve and Adam, these disciples indicate that the seed of the woman would take precedence over any reinstatement of the monarchy. Given Jeremiah's tendency to favor the time before the establishment of the monarchy when the roles of men and women were much more egalitarian, this reference to the seed of the woman very well could be a metaphor for this preference. If such is the case, then in this

5. Brueggemann, "From Dust to Kingship," 2.

story, Yahweh is portrayed as the one who indicates that women once again would have a more prominent role in the future governance of the people.

THE CONSEQUENCES FOR THE WOMAN

With the establishment and institutionalization of the monarchy, much of what Yahweh had warned the people would happen by choosing a king for themselves had come true. First of all, the pain of giving birth would increase for women. As a predominantly agrarian society prior to the monarchy, the harshness of the environment contributed to the rate of infant mortality that always would cause women to experience the pain of losing a child at birth or of having an infant die in the early years of her or his life. This dynamic would continue even with the establishment of the monarchy. However, there would be an increase in the infant mortality rate as a result of several other factors under the monarchy: the impoverishment and indebtedness of farmers who would have to subject their children to the harsh reality of slavery in order to pay their debts; the institution of child sacrifice endorsed and promoted by the monarchy; the conscription of young men into the king's military; and the death of children as a result of the king's offensive campaign against a neighboring nation or the king's aggressive defense against a threatening nation, both of which would invite hostile retaliation and the violent death of many innocent children throughout the land.

The siege and subsequent conquest by the Babylonians proved to be a tragic culmination of this aggressive defensiveness on the part of the monarchy. Jeremiah had warned Zedekiah repeatedly not to take up arms against the mighty Babylonians. Jeremiah was very clear about what would happen to the sons and daughters of the land if Zedekiah would not establish a treaty with the Babylonians. Complicated by the occurrence of a famine at the same time that Jerusalem was besieged, everything that Jeremiah had predicted would happen to the children of the land came true because King Zedekiah decided to resist and fight against the Babylonians.

The children of the land perished as a result of the famine and the conquest. The bodies of children became like food for the animals, as well as for the people who were still alive in the besieged city of Jerusalem. No one could have imagined what pain the mothers of the land must have felt as they watched their children die before their very eyes, and then be used for food to feed the starving population. With such a weakened population, once the Babylonians were able to break through the walls of the city, the slaughter of the children and the killing of sons who were fighting for King Zedekiah happened very quickly. As Jeremiah had warned, the people did not even have time to bury their children, whom they had to leave on the ground like the dung of an animal. Any woman who became pregnant during this time or who gave birth to a child certainly knew the pain of bringing a child into this situation that almost guaranteed certain death for the infant.

During the course of this inquiry, occasionally I would ask women, "What, in your opinion, would be the source of greater pain—the actual physical pain of giving birth to your child or the pain of knowing that within the first 5 years of your child's life, your child would most likely die as the result of the social, economic, or political conditions into which your child was being born?" Almost to a woman, everyone acknowledged that the pain associated with the latter situation would be much greater than the physical pain associated with giving birth. Granted, all of these women were from the twenty-first century and living comfortably in the United States, but their responses were very informative about what I would consider to be a universal answer in comparing these two sources of pain in a woman's life.

Although most scholars identify the pain described in this verse (Gen 3:16) as the physical pain of giving birth to a child, I would suggest that given the experience of Jeremiah and his disciples during the reign of Josiah to Zedekiah and the horror of the conquest of Jerusalem by the Babylonians, this reference to the pain that women experience in giving birth to a child is a description about the increase of the infant and child mortality rate that resulted from the religious, economic, and military policies of the monarchy. Yet, even with all of these policies that put the life of a child in jeopardy, the women of Israel and Judah still desired to have intercourse with their husbands.

Another dynamic that changed under the monarchy was the role, responsibility, and status of women. Prior to the establishment of the monarchy, women had a much more prominent role and responsibility in the welfare of the family and society, and they were accorded the respect that was associated with such involvement and investment in the decisions of the people. However, with the establishment of the monarchy, the men of the land assumed more and more authority and power in determining the course of society, while the authority and power of women was diminished to the point that women were considered and treated as second-class citizens. Kings were usually male. Officials of the royal court and military officers were usually male. Prophets and priests were usually male. Wealthy landowners were usually male. With the institution of the monarchy, the hierarchy of society was redefined such that women became more and more subject to the authority and power of men.[6] This shift also carried over into the relationship between husbands and wives. Husbands now had royal permission, so to speak, to rule over their wives in ways that previous to the monarchy may have been less common. Given the perspective and prejudice of Jeremiah and his disciples, this shift from the more equitable relationship that had existed between men and women in society prior to the monarchy was yet another negative result of the monarchy that proved detrimental to the well-being of society for everyone involved.

THE CURSE ON THE GROUND

Under the monarchy, some men fared no better than the women. As Yahweh had warned the people, when they decided to have a king like other nations, the king would favor some men over others in society. The king also would requisition the best of the harvest of plants and animals from the farmers throughout the land as a form of taxation. This policy and practice placed an undue burden upon those who owned little land or produced crops and raised herds for their own sustenance. When farmers and herdsmen were unable to meet the king's demands, they would become indebted to the king and then be forced to sell their land to a wealthy landowner in order to pay off their debt. Eventually they would have to borrow money in order to farm their land. If they could not pay off their debt, then they would be forced to become slaves of the wealthy landowner until the debt was paid. Under these circumstances, a man would work as a slave by the sweat of his face in order to build a summer or winter house for someone else to inhabit or to plant a vineyard for someone else to reap the profit, all the while barely being able to earn a living for himself and his family. Both Israel and Judah would toil under this institution of slavery until both tribes would be decimated and destroyed,

---

6. Scanzoni, *All We're Meant to Be*, 64.

returning to the apparent nothingness from which they originated when they were chosen by Yahweh to be a royal people in Yahweh's sight.

According to the prophetic imagination of Jeremiah and his disciples, as a result of all of the evil that the kings of Israel and Judah had done in the sight of Yahweh, both nations had been relegated to the paltry dust of non-existence—Israel being conquered by the Assyrians, and Judah being conquered by the Babylonians. For those people from Israel and Judah who were deported to other parts of the world to till the soil and tend the animals of the field because the kings of these two nations had presumed to rule as if divine, all seemed to be lost as they were driven out of their land to destinations east of their lush and fertile land that was so much a part of their identity.

THE TREE OF LIFE

However, all was not lost, for there remained in this lush and fertile land a tree of life—the sign of hope that one day they would return to their land and be able to recapture the life that was much more favorable and peaceful before the time when the evil will of the people had won the day and they had decided to have a king like other nations. Hopefully, upon their return, they would have learned their lesson well. One way that they could make sure that this lesson would not be forgotten would be to tell this story to their descendents so that no one ever again would choose a government like the monarchy in which kings acted as if they were gods while causing an increase in the mortality of infants and children, greater subjugation of women, and the enslavement of men and their families throughout the land.

Several lenses have been used in order to offer this particular interpretation of the story of Eve and Adam. The first lens is historical. Drawing upon the extensive reconstructed narrative of the Deuteronomistic historians, the followers of Jeremiah have summarized this history for their own purpose—to critique a monarchy that they deemed to be responsible for the demise of both Israel and Judah. The second lens is political. In constructive prophetic fashion, this story is used not only to expose the apparent consequences of a corrupt, oppressive, and violent government, but also to offer a word of hope in the face of such pain, suffering, and death. The third lens is metaphorical. Although the main characters of this story—Eve, Adam and the serpent—are never mentioned by name in the book of Jeremiah, the linguistic comparison of this story with the book of Jeremiah reveals that Eve and Adam are strong metaphors for Israel and Judah. The serpent is a metaphor for the monarchy which was established because the people wanted to have a king like other nations—a monarchy that ultimately was reduced to nothingness as it was subjected to eat dust for the rest of its existence.

Clearly, the parallel reading from Isa 65:17–25 has been very helpful in developing this interpretation of the story of Eve and Adam. The reference to the serpent whose food shall be dust has been particularly beneficial in seeing the story of Eve and Adam from an historical and political perspective. Like Jeremiah and his followers, the authors of Third Isaiah viewed the former monarchs as blind, ignorant, corrupt, and self-indulgent. What appears to be of utmost importance to the disciples of Isaiah is the restoration of the reign of Yahweh throughout the land in which Yahweh's law of justice and righteousness would replace the oppression, devastation, and violence that filled the land under the previous monarchy.

The disciples of Jeremiah were more practical. Their presentation of the unity of Eve and Adam prior to the appearance of the serpent indicates a desire to return to some semblance of governance that was operative for Israel and Judah prior to the establishment of the monarchy when these two nations co-existed peacefully, and men and women shared in the responsibility of leadership among the people. In order to ensure that their descendents are persuaded to pursue this way of life, these disciples emphasize that they are never to reinstate any form of government like the monarchy that was responsible for bringing so much pain and suffering upon its own people.

Incorporating this message into the genre of a creation story is indicative of the imagination of the prophet. What appears to be a story of creation and an explanation for the origin of life simply is a convenient context for these disciples of Jeremiah to warn the descendents of Israel and Judah never to return to the monarchy that did so much evil to its own people in the sight of Yahweh. The exposure to all of the ancient creation stories of Babylon served these disciples well as an inspiration for using this genre of a creation story in conveying their primary message that they thought to be of utmost importance for all future generations.

Having come to this discovery and conclusion about the authorship and purpose of the story of Eve and Adam, I was left wondering, "Could the same lenses of history, politics, and metaphor also be used to interpret the first story in Genesis?" If so, then these lenses also could offer a new understanding about the priests' primary message of this first story in Genesis that would coincide with the purpose for telling the story of Eve and Adam (see Appendix). Such a correlation would only lend greater credibility to the interpretation of the story of Eve and Adam presented in this book.

Conclusion

WHAT STARTED OUT FOR me as a simple question about the meaning of the pain associated with giving birth that is mentioned in Gen 3:16 evolved into a full-blown inquiry and discovery about the authorship and purpose of this story of Eve and Adam. I did not begin this journey with some hypothesis about this story that I had to prove or disprove. However, once I opened the door to the possibility that this story was grounded in the historical experience of Israel and Judah, I saw for the first time in my life that this story of Eve and Adam appeared to be a synopsis of the history of Israel and Judah from the time that they co-existed as two nations supposedly in a land of delight to the time that the people of Judah were deported to Babylon. Based upon this observation, I concluded that the author or authors of this story had to be someone who had lived through this horrendous experience or who had learned about it from those who had survived the conquest and deportation by the Babylonians.

The main assumption that I have made throughout this inquiry is based upon the conclusion by Rainer Albertz that the leadership of the people following their return from Babylon consisted of a council of priests as well as the Deuteronomistic reformers which included many of the disciples of the prophet Jeremiah. Considering that these two groups were responsible at the time for gathering and compiling much of the literature that had been written in the aftermath of the conquest, deportation, and return, I realized that these two parties could have been the authors of the two stories at the beginning of the Hebrew Scriptures. Albertz and others make a strong argument for the fact that Jeremiah and his disciples were devout advocates for the worship of Yahweh and would be considered Yahwists in the best sense of that title. If such is the case, then this information is consistent with what I learned earlier in my life about the authorship of these two stories—the first story in Genesis reflecting the priestly tradition and the second story reflecting the Yahwist tradition.

Like everyone else in the aftermath of the conquest and deportation by the Babylonians, the priests and these reformers also had to answer the question, "Where did we go wrong?" Once I viewed the story of Eve and Adam through the lens of this question, I realized that this story provided a definite answer to this question. For centuries, the prophets had been such strong critics of the monarchy, and this prophetic critique continued as the disciples of Jeremiah situated this imaginative story within the genre of a creation story in order to accomplish their purpose for writing this story—to dissuade their people for generations to come from reinstating the monarchy that formerly had been responsible for so much painful oppression, slavery, and death among the people of Israel and Judah.

The interpretation offered in this book is dependent upon the perspective that Eve and Adam are metaphors for Israel and Judah. That Eve and Adam hardly are mentioned by name in the rest of the Hebrew Scriptures raises significant questions about the importance of these two characters in all of the theological literature that was being written during the time of the deportation of people from Judah to Babylon and the return of the people to their homeland some fifty years later. However, references to both Israel and Judah throughout the historical accounts, the prophets, and the writings of the Hebrew Scriptures are so constant and consistent that anyone hearing this story of Eve and Adam in the context of all of this literary explosion presumably would understand that these two characters were metaphors for these two nations.

The question that still haunts me is one for which I have no answer. If Eve and Adam are metaphors for Israel and Judah as I have presented in this book, then why is this metaphor not mentioned in the rabbinic discourse recorded from 200 BCE on or in the testimony of Jesus and the Apostle Paul in the Christian writings? What happened during this period of time that caused people to focus on Eve and Adam as real people or as personifications of all women and men? Certainly the records and testimonies from 200 BCE and later have played a strong influence in how we have read and interpreted this story for two millennia. The subsequent emphases and interpretations of this story by people such as Augustine and Luther have served only to solidify this perspective that Eve and Adam were real people or personifications of all women and men who were created without sin, but who, by their own disobedience, fell into sin and suffered the consequences.

Despite all of the theological literature that has been written based upon this dominant interpretation of this illustrious story—either in agreement or disagreement—I have offered you another perspective of this story for your consideration. What I have discovered and concluded from my inquiry about the authorship and purpose of this story during the past twenty years makes the most sense to me out of any interpretation that has been presented during the past 2200 years. As each piece of this inquiry fell into place, I became more and more convinced that this story of Eve and Adam was written by the disciples of Jeremiah to persuade their people and all of their descendants that reinstating the monarchy would be a big mistake, and probably would result in the increase of infant and child mortality, greater subjugation of women, and the enslavement of their own people as happened under the previous monarchy.

Rather than providing an explanation for the creation of the universe, the formation of human beings, the institution of marriage, the origin of sin in this world, the serpent crawling on its belly, the physical pain of childbirth, the subjugation of women, the need for men to labor in order to earn a living, the existence of death in this life, or the priority of creation over evolution, this story of Eve and Adam offers a strong critique of a monarchy that caused a hostile division between two formerly cooperative nations. Both the monarchy of Israel and the monarchy of Judah created an environment in which women would have to anticipate that the children to whom they would give birth would die prematurely, women would be dominated by their husbands as well as by all men in society, and people would have to serve the king and his wealthy supporters as slaves. Under the guise of being a servant of Yahweh, the king chose to behave like a god unto himself and ultimately was responsible for the demise of both of these nations.

What I have suggested with this historical, political, and metaphorical interpretation of this imaginative story of Eve and Adam is an interpretation that not only is reflective of a particular historical experience, but also is applicable for every generation. No government is without its faults, but one of the best ways to evaluate any government is to examine the infant mortality rate, the treatment of women, and the enslavement of any people that serve to keep the government in power. The disciples of Jeremiah developed and used these same three criteria in their story of

Eve and Adam not only to critique the former monarchy, but also to advocate for a government in which these painful experiences of corporate life would be minimized, if not eliminated altogether. Drawing upon this prophetic critique, I would suggest that if the policy and practice of any government contributes to the infant and child mortality throughout the land, perpetuates the subjugation of women in society, or creates conditions that enslave any citizen in any way, then this government has failed to serve its people and ought to be challenged to change its policy and practice or be replaced by a form of governance that is more committed to the justice, peace, and freedom of everyone throughout the land.

At this point, I have to return to the verse with which I started this inquiry—Gen 3:16. Now, more than ever, I am convinced that the pain referenced in this verse does not refer primarily to the physical pain of giving birth, but rather to the deep pain that a woman feels because she knows that the infant to whom she is giving birth probably will die very early in her or his life as the result of the political and economic conditions of the day that the infant was born. Most of the interpretations of this pronouncement by God have presumed that a woman is destined to experience physical pain in giving birth to a child, no matter whether the pain is prescriptive for all women, or descriptive of the reality that all women experience. My encounter with the women of N Street Village helped me to see that this pain in Gen 3:16 is neither prescriptive nor descriptive, but rather is very conditional based upon the way that any governing authority rules over the people of a nation. Evidence of this pain spans the globe as well as exposes the painful oppression and violence in our own land.

No matter whether a government is democratic, autocratic, or socialist, whenever a governing authority perceives that it is ordained by God to act in God's stead, many of the citizens of the nation are bound to suffer. Such rulers pretend to be like gods who think that they can exercise their authority and power over people for the sole purpose of establishing and preserving their own reign. In order to secure their position, governing authorities will wage wars against other rulers under the disguise of a divine mandate, while depriving their own people of the basic necessities of life and demanding the greatest sacrifice from those who are the most poor or vulnerable in the land.

As authors of this story of Eve and Adam, the disciples of Jeremiah not only offered a critique of the monarchy, but also advocated subtly for a practical form of government that they thought would benefit all of the people of the land and avoid the failures of the former monarchy. Based upon this story, we can imagine that they were calling for the establishment of a more egalitarian form of governance similar to the one that had existed prior to the monarchy. This form of governance would be more reflective of the justice and peace desired by Yahweh and would result in much less infant mortality, subjugation of women, and enslavement of their own people.

Under the monarchy, too many infants and children had died prematurely and unnecessarily due to the aspirations of the king, the women of the land had been relegated to a much lesser role in their society, and those who were impoverished throughout the land were forced to work as slaves in order to cater to the ambitions of the king and his loyal entourage. The disciples of Jeremiah wanted to reverse this trend. In the void left by the demise of the monarchy, they were in a position to exercise their own authority and power and state their preference for a more egalitarian form of government that was much less patriarchal and would restore the respectful right of women to have some say in the management of their community. If their descendents could strive for this form of governance, then hopefully the amount of infant and child mortality could be reduced significantly and the land could be restored to a place that was meant to be a peaceful delight for everyone who would be born and dwell in this Garden of Eden.

Appendix

The Lens of the Priests

For most of my life, I have been taught that the first story in Genesis, commonly known as the seven-day creation story, came out of the priestly tradition. If so, then Albertz's proposal that the priests were partners with the Deuteronomistic reformers in governing their people in the post-exilic period provides an historical context for their contribution to this instructive narrative at the beginning of their sacred scriptures. Like their counterparts, these priests would have been asking the same question that had plagued most of their people following the conquest of Jerusalem by the Babylonians and the deportation to Babylon. What had the nations of Israel and Judah done wrong to bring about all of the oppression, violence, and devastation that the people had suffered for centuries?

Looking at this seven-day story through the lens of this question, for the first time in my life I saw that everything in this story leads up to the seventh day, which is a metaphor for the Sabbath day—a day that was supposed to be remembered and kept holy by the people of Israel and Judah. As they looked back on all that had transpired under the monarchy, these priests realized that their people had failed to keep the Sabbath day holy, beginning with the kings of Israel and Judah, and spreading throughout the people of both of these nations. In order to impress upon their descendents how important this holy day was for their future survival, these priests also used the genre of a creation story and placed this story at the very beginning of all of the literature that they were compiling. In this way, the priests indicated to their people that this Sabbath day was instituted by God at the very beginning of time as a way of ensuring the justice and peace that God desired for the entire world.

A perusal of all of the literature related to this first chapter of Genesis reveals the bias of our humanity. Assuming that this story was intended to explain the origin of a universe that was created by God, the vast majority of our literature concentrates on the sixth day when God created the first human beings in the image of God who commanded them to be fruitful and multiply and have dominion over the face of the earth. Given the wealth of literature devoted to this sixth day of creation, the amount of literature that delves into the importance of the seventh day is like a footnote to the rest of the story. Using the same lenses of history, politics, and metaphor, I have come to the conclusion that the entire purpose for the priests telling this story and placing it at the very beginning of all of the literature that they were compiling at this time was to stress the importance of remembering the Sabbath day and keeping this day holy in order to avoid much of the oppression, corruption, and violence that they had suffered under the monarchy.

According to the Hebrew Scriptures, the Sabbath day involved much more than a day of rest from all of the labor of the other six days of the week. The Sabbath day also included all of the sabbatical practices that culminated in the year of the Jubilee as described in the book of Leviticus. These practices included giving the land a rest every seven years, giving slaves the option to go free, cancelling debts, and ultimately returning property to the family that owned that land fifty years previously. After experiencing all of the oppression, corruption, and violence under the monarchy and the devastation caused by the Babylonians, these priests came to the conclusion that had they remembered the Sabbath day and kept it holy, their people could have avoided so much of the suffering and pain in their lives that resulted from deciding to have a king like all the other nations.

As far as anyone can tell, the remembrance of the Sabbath day occurred very seldom during the monarchy. However, when the people were deported to Babylon, the observance of the Sabbath day took on much greater importance in the lives of the people. In the absence of the monarchy, suddenly the priests were free to guide the people in the way of justice and righteousness as they preferred. Looking back on their experience under the monarchy, these priests became aware that had this observance of the Sabbath day been in force during the monarchy, much of the disparity, poverty, oppression, slavery, exploitation, and land monopoly that happened under the previous form of government could have been avoided. Now that the people had returned home and were faced with the decision of determining how they would be governed in the future and what policies would be enacted to accomplish God's justice and righteousness throughout the land, the priests were in the position of authority and power to make sure that all of the oppression, corruption, and violence that happened under the monarchy would never happen again.

The priests who were part of the governing council that was guiding the people during this time of resettlement in their homeland took advantage of their position and developed this story about God's creation of the earth in seven days in order to accentuate the importance of keeping the Sabbath day holy. Given all of the exposure that the priests had to the Babylonian creation stories while in Babylon, this genre of communication was fresh on their minds. However, they would write their own story utilizing this genre of a creation story, not for the purpose of explaining the origin of life on this planet, but rather for the purpose of depicting God's establishment of the Sabbath day in the beginning of time so that their people would realize the importance of this holy day and incorporate all of the sabbatical practices in their daily lives for the sake of everyone being able to experience the justice, peace, and freedom that God desired for everyone throughout the land.

As with the story of Eve and Adam, the variety of interpretations of this seven-day creation story is innumerable. I have no desire to examine all of these interpretations, other than to state that this story probably was not written with the primary intention of explaining the origin of the heavens, the earth, the day, the night, the waters, the sky, the plants, the sun, the moon, the birds, the fish, the animals, and human beings. Given the progression of this story, everything leads up to the seventh day when God rested from all of the labor that God had done during the previous six days. So God blessed the seventh day and hallowed it, because on this day, God rested.

Remembering this seventh day, which is a metaphor for the Sabbath day, and keeping this day holy was viewed by the priests as the most critical practice that could guarantee a much more justice-oriented and egalitarian society in the future and bring about the peace and prosperity envisioned by so many of the prophets of Israel and Judah. If the people would be faithful in honoring this day, so much of the corruption and violence that occurred under the monarchy could be avoided. No more oppressive taxation. No more indebtedness that forces people to forfeit their land and become tenant farmers. No more slavery until a person paid off a debt, which seldom happened. No more long-term monopoly of land ownership by wealthy landowners. No more need for a strong military to protect the wealthy landowners and keep the people from rebelling against whoever ruled the land.

Given the amount of literature devoted to the sixth day of this story, especially in terms of how human beings are supposed to have dominion over every living thing on the face of this earth, I would suggest that the priests' description of the seventh day offers a powerful prescription, not only for justice and peace throughout their land, but also for the care of the entire earth. In this regard, the priests have offered their own critique of the monarchy which for too long had dominated, oppressed, and enslaved their own people and waged wars that only caused more suffering and pain for everyone throughout their land. I would conclude that these priests had very little interest in conjecturing about the origin of life on this planet. They wrote this story because of their commitment to remembering the Sabbath day and keeping this day holy, which makes the seventh day, including all of the sabbatical practices associated with this day, not a footnote, but rather the exclamation point to this story.

Bibliography

Aalders, G. Charles. *Genesis*. Grand Rapids: Zondervan, 1981.
Albertz, Rainer. *A History of Israelite Religion in the Old Testament Period*. 2 vols. Translated by John Bowden. Louisville: Westminster John Knox, 1994.
———. *Israel in Exile: The History and Literature of the Sixth Century BCE*. Translated by David Green. Studies in Biblical Literature 3. Atlanta: Society of Biblical Literature, 2003.
Anderson, Gary. *The Genesis of Perfection: Adam and Eve in Jewish and Christian Imagination*. Louisville: Westminster John Knox, 2001.
Asimov, Isaac. *In the Beginning....* New York: Crown, 1981.
Bechtel, Lyn. "Rethinking the Interpretation of Genesis 2:4b—3:24." In *A Feminist Companion to Genesis*, edited by Athalya Brenner, 77–117. Sheffield: Sheffield Academic, 1993.
Bellis, Alice. *Helpmates, Harlots and Heroes: Women's Stories in the Hebrew Bible*. Louisville: Westminster John Knox, 1994.
Bledstein, Adrien. "Are Women Cursed in Genesis 3:16?" In *A Feminist Companion to Genesis*, edited by Athalya Brenner, 142–45. Sheffield: Sheffield Academic, 1993.
Bloom, Harold, and David Rosenberg, *The Book of J*. New York: Grove Weidenfeld, 1990.
Boice, James. *Genesis*. Grand Rapids: Zondervan, 1982.
Brown, William. *The Ethos of the Cosmos: The Genesis of Moral Imagination in the Bible*. Grand Rapids: Eerdmans, 1999.
Brueggemann, Walter. "From Dust to Kingship." *Zeitschrift für die alttestamentliche Wissenschaft* 84 (1972) 1–18.
———. *Genesis: A Bible Commentary for Teaching and Preaching*. Interpretation. Atlanta: John Knox, 1982.
———. *Old Testament Theology: Essays on Structure, Theme and Text*. Edited by Patrick D. Miller. Minneapolis: Fortress, 1992.
———. *Texts Under Construction: The Bible and Postmodern Imagination*. Minneapolis: Fortress, 1993.
———. *Theology of the Old Testament: Testimony, Dispute, Advocacy*. Minneapolis: Fortress, 1997.
Cassuto, Umberto. *A Commentary on the Book of Genesis*. Translated by Israel Abrahams. Jerusalem: Magnes, 1944.
Clines, David J. A. *What Does Eve Do to Help? And Other Readerly Questions to the Old Testament*. Journal for the Study of the Old Testament Supplements 94. Sheffield: Sheffield Academic, 1990.
Conklin, Edward. *Getting Back into the Garden of Eden*. Lanham, MD: University Press of America, Inc., 1998.

Coote Robert B., and David Robert Ord. *The Bible's First History*. Philadelphia: Fortress, 1989.

Cropp, Robert, et al. *People of the Covenant: An Introduction to the Old Testament*. New York: Oxford University Press, 1988.

Davies, John. *Beginning Now: Contemporary Experience of Creation and Fall*. London: Collins, 1971.

Davies, Philip, and John Rogerson. *The Old Testament World*. Englewood Cliffs, NJ: Prentice Hall, 1989.

Delumeau, Jean. *History of Paradise: The Garden of Eden in Myth and Tradition*. Translated by Matthew O'Connell. New York: Continuum, 1995.

Eakin, Frank. *The Religion and Cultures of Israel: An Introduction to Old Testament Thought*. Boston: Allyn & Bacon, 1971.

Ellis, Peter. *The Yahwist: The Bible's First Theologian*. Collegeville, MN: Liturgical, 1968.

Fewell, Danna Nolan, and David M. Gunn. *Gender, Power and Promise: The Subject of the Bible's First Story*. Nashville: Abingdon, 1993.

Foh, Susan. "What is the Woman's Desire?" *Westminster Theological Journal* 37 (1975) 376–83.

Fretheim, Terence. *Creation, Fall and Flood: Studies in Genesis 1–11*. Minneapolis: Augsburg, 1969.

Gardner, Anne. "Genesis 2:4b–3: A Mythological Paradigm of Sexual Equality or of the Religious History of Pre-exilic Israel?" *Scottish Journal of Theology* 43 (1990) 1–18.

Gnuse, Robert. *No Other Gods: Emergent Monotheism in Israel*. Journal for the Study of the Old Testament Supplements 241. Sheffield: Sheffield Academic, 1997.

Gowan, Donald. *From Eden to Babel: A Commentary on the Book of Genesis 1–11*. Grand Rapids: Eerdmans, 1988.

———. *When Man Becomes God: Humanism and Hybris in the Old Testament*. Pittsburgh: Pickwick, 1975.

Grabbe, Lester, editor. *Leading Captivity Captive: 'The Exile' as History and Ideology*. Journal for the Study of the Old Testament Supplements 278. Sheffield: Sheffield Academic, 1998.

Habel, Norman C. *The Form and Meaning of the Fall Narrative: A Detailed Analysis of Genesis 3*. St. Louis: Concordia Seminary Press Shop, 1965.

Hammar, Margaret. *Giving Birth: Reclaiming Biblical Metaphor for Pastoral Practice*. Louisville: Westminster John Knox, 1994.

Hayter, Mary. *The New Eve in Christ*. Grand Rapids: Eerdmans, 1987.

Hiebert, Theodore. *The Yahwist's Landscape: Nature and Religion in Early Israel*. New York: Oxford University Press, 1996.

Jones, Douglas. *Isaiah 56–66 and Joel: Introduction and Commentary*. Torch Bible Commentaries. London: SCM, 1964.

Kass, Leon R. *The Beginning of Wisdom: Reading Genesis*. New York: Free Press, 2003.

Kennedy, James. "Peasants in Revolt: Political Allegory in Genesis 2–3." *Journal for the Study of the Old Testament* 47 (1990) 3–14.

Knight, George A. F. *The New Israel: A Commentary on the Book of Isaiah 56–66*. International Theological Commentary. Grand Rapids: Eerdmans, 1985.

Kvam, Kristen E, editors. *Eve and Adam: Jewish, Christian, and Muslim Readings on Genesis and Gender*. Bloomington: Indiana University Press, 1999.

Lemche, Niels Peter. *The Israelites in History and Tradition*. Library of Ancient Israel. Louisville: Westminster John Knox, 1999.

Leupold, H. C. *Exposition of Genesis*. Grand Rapids: Baker, 1942.
Levenson, Jon D. *The Death and Resurrection of the Beloved Son: The Transformation of Child Sacrifice in Judaism and Christianity*. New Haven: Yale University Press, 1993.
L'Heureaux, Conrad E. *In and Out of Paradise*. New York: Paulist, 1983.
Luther, Martin. *Luther's Works: Lectures on Genesis*. Translated by George Schick. St. Louis: Concordia, 1958.
Luttikhuizen, Gerard P., editor. *The Creation of Man and Woman: Interpretations of the Biblical Narrative in Jewish and Christian Traditions*. Themes in Biblical Narrative 3. Leiden: Brill, 2000.
McBride, S. Dean. "Biblical Literature in its Historical Context: The Old Testament." In *Harper's Bible Commentary*, edited by James L. Mays, 14–24. San Francisco: Harper & Row, 1988.
McNutt, Paula. *Reconstructing the Society of Ancient Israel*. Library of Ancient Israel. Louisville: Westminster John Knox, 1999.
Mendalhall, George. "The Shady Side of Wisdom: The Date and Purpose of Genesis 3." In *A Light unto My Path: Old Testament Studies in Honor of Jacob M. Myers*, edited by Howard N. Bream, et al., 319–34. Gettysburg Theological Studies 4. Philadelphia: Temple University Press, 1974.
Meyers, Carol. *Discovering Eve: Ancient Israelite Women in Context*. New York: Oxford University Press, 1988.
———. "Gender Roles and Genesis 3:16 Revisited." In *A Feminist Companion to Genesis*, edited by Athalya Brenner, 118–41. Feminist Companion to the Bible 2. Sheffield: Sheffield Academic, 1993.
———. "Women and the Domestic Economy of Early Israel." In *Women in the Hebrew Bible: A Reader*, edited by Alice Bach, 33–43. New York: Routledge, 1999.
Ottosson, Magness. "Eden and the Land of Promise." In *Congress Volume: Jerusalem, 1986*, edited by J. A. Emerton, 176–88. Vetus Testamentum Supplements 40. Leiden: Brill, 1988.
Pagels, Elaine. *Adam, Eve and the Serpent*. New York: Random House, 1988.
Phillips, John. *Eve: The History of an Idea*. San Francisco: Harper & Row, 1984.
Phipps, William. *Genesis and Gender: Biblical Myths of Sexuality and Their Cultural Impact*. New York: Praeger, 1989.
Rosenberg, Joel. *King and Kin: Political Allegory in the Hebrew Bible*. Indiana Studies in Biblical Literature. Indianapolis: Indiana University Press, 1986.
Ross, Allen. *Creation and Blessing: A Guide to the Study and Exposition of Genesis*. Grand Rapids: Baker, 1988.
Sarna, Nahum. *Genesis*. JPS Torah Commentary. Philadelphia: Jewish Publication Society, 1989.
Scanzoni, Letha, and Nancy Hardesty. *All We're Meant to Be: Biblical Feminism for Today*. Grand Rapids: Eerdmans, 1992.
Schmidt, Werner. "A Theologian of the Solomonic Era? A Plea for the Yahwist." In *Studies in the Period of David and Solomon and Other Essays*, edited by Tomoo Ishida, 53–73. Winona Lake, IN: Eisenbrauns, 1982.
Schungel-Strauman, Helen. "Creation of Man and Woman." In *A Feminist Companion to Genesis*, edited by Athalya Brenner, 67–72. Feminist Companion to the Bible 2. Sheffield: Sheffield Academic, 1993.
Scullion, John. *Genesis: A Commentary for Students, Teachers and Preachers*. Collegeville, MN: Liturgical, 1992.

Smith, Daniel L. *The Religion of the Landless: The Social Context of the Babylonian Exile.* Bloomington, IN: Meyer-Stone, 1989.

Smith, Mark. *The Early History of God: Yahweh and the Other Deities in Ancient Israel.* San Francisco: Harper & Row, 1990.

Soelle, Dorothee. *The Strength of the Weak: Toward a Christian Feminist Identity.* Philadelphia: Westminster, 1984.

Stigers, Harold. *A Commentary on Genesis.* Grand Rapids: Zondervan, 1976.

Stordalen, Terje. *Echoes of Eden: Genesis 2–3 and Symbolism of the Eden Garden in Biblical Hebrew Literature.* Leuven: Peeters, 2000.

Thompson, Thomas L. *The Mythic Past: Biblical Archaeology and the Myth of Israel.* New York: Basic Books, 1998.

Trible, Phyllis. *God and the Rhetoric of Sexuality.* Overtures to Biblical Theology. Philadelphia: Fortress, 1998.

Van Seters, John. *Prologue to History: The Yahwist as Historian in Genesis.* Louisville: Westminster John Knox, 1992.

Vawter, Bruce. *On Genesis: A New Reading.* New York: Doubleday, 1977.

Westermann, Claus. *Genesis 1–11: A Commentary.* Translated by J. J. Scullion. Continental Commentaries. Minneapolis: Augsburg, 1984.

Winnett, Frederick. "Re-examining the Foundations." *Journal of Biblical Literature* 84 (1965) 1–14.